Also available:

Intelligent Lessons of Music Knowledge (Guitar and Piano) Volume I
Intelligent Lessons of Music Knowledge (Guitar and Piano) Volume II
and
Piccadilly by Larissa Houghton

INTELLIGENT LESSONS of MUSIC KNOWLEDGE (GUITAR AND PIANO) VOLUME III

Mary Sewall

INTELLIGENT LESSONS OF MUSIC KNOWLEDGE
(GUITAR AND PIANO) VOLUME III

iUniverse books may be ordered through booksellers or by contacting:

iUniverse LLC
1663 Liberty Drive
Bloomington, IN 47403
www.iuniverse.com
1-800-Authors (1-800-288-4677)

ISBN: 978-1-4917-4007-1 (sc)
ISBN: 978-1-4917-4008-8 (e)

Printed in the United States of America.

iUniverse rev. date: 8/6/2014

CONTENTS

GUITAR AND PIANO 1

MINOR KEYS...6

MUSIC IN THE MINOR KEY 12

TRANSPOSING 21

STEPHEN FOSTER COLLINS...32

STYLE 40

STRUCTURE OF THE E BAR CHORDS..50

CHORD CHART FOR GUITAR 60

A SHAPE BAR CHORDS 69

CIRCLE OF FIFTHS 76

ABOUT THE AUTHOR 89

CHAPTER ONE

*****

LESSON 1

GUITAR AND PIANO

How great to be back with all my musicians. It seems the economy is only getting worse, and probably will continue with this bleak and dismal situation. This state of affairs and its consequence is affecting the world. It is difficult to continue acting as though all is well. Certainly this New Year, with all of its gigantic problematic thrust, burst into a world that boggles the mind. But, Darlings do your best to stay afloat.

One way is to keep your mind agile, and open the door to the great minds of all times. We are not alone. The great musicians of the past centuries are still with us. They live on stronger than ever. Their lives on the earth were but a moment long, but the music lives on forever. Let us gather this knowledge and reap the reward from it.

Be careful, do not be a "Jack of All Trades." Zero in on one career, and give it your all, and it will last a life time. Need you ask for anything more! The rewards will keep you in good stead. Music is far- reaching. Greater than you can imagine, if however, you want to add it to your busy schedule, and you already have a career, then it is a matter of starting slowly. Prepare ahead of time: The life you have now will eventually come to a close, as in retirement. With music, that door remains open, and never closes.

This is true: Music is eternal. If the body is not as agile as it once was, then the brain continues with the task at hand. Many Great Music Conductors learn their whole scores of Operas, Symphonic Compositions, and so forth away from the instruments. This way the physical body could be at rest.

In this Vol. 3, we will continue in our quest for knowledge. When I lived in Queens, New York, and attended the various Music Schools, I was thirsty for certain aspects of my instrument, and also how to better understand, and develop as I progressed along. For some reason, I felt the knowledge that was available wasn't satisfying enough. It didn't keep in step in the proper sequence. There were too many empty spaces that seemed out of line. That was very disturbing.

This reminds me of a friend who wanted to learn how to operate the computer. She enrolled in a course, and was immediately supplied with a ton of books on the subject. This overwhelmed her so completely she felt helpless over the crush, and walked away from it never to return again.

With music it is much worse, as the computer doesn't go back in time like the piano or the guitar. We are talking centuries of knowledge to the present age. To present something of this magnitude, to break it down to be understandable, without the student losing the interest as it moves along. How many teachers have the ability to impart the information?

Many teachers don't have an inkling of what they are talking about. However, a bright student seems to have the talent to overcome this deficiency. But, why should it be where many teachers happen to be dunces in this respect. I believe I have the answer! Music teachers are not regulated. They do not have to pass a State Examination for qualifications to teach. That would mean many so-called "Teachers" are running around without the proper knowledge. So the "Motto of the Story" is to know the background and training of the selected expert.

Well Darlings, enough of the chit-chat, and digressing from our main topic. Let us now do some actual work from one of the books of a complete set. When first starting lessons, or when a number of books have been acquired during the process of lessons with a number of teachers, do not hesitant to look them over carefully. Once a music book has been completed, and put aside never to be opened again, thinking nothing more can be gained from it, because the instructor continues with the next one in order.

This is when the interest is peaked, whether you realize or not. Going through the various books the first time around is but a teaser. Not much is actually absorbed. There is a wealth of material left behind. When first introduced only a small portion is assimilated, and before the mind could digest, and think over and accept, and become part of the person, the new material is clogged in and becomes a hindrance, not an asset.

Of course, it is exciting to open the new book. The crisp crinkly pages are a thrill to be peered at and see all the new pieces ready to be played. But like a child with a new toy it soon becomes boring. The reason for that: because, being the next stage, it is beyond reach for the pupil, and many times the end is in sight for any future lessons.

Keeping up with the various stages of the music has a lot to do with the instructor. There are so many factors involved: understanding the material, the interest, and so forth. With some everything is in place, and a happy session takes place. But, alas, no two pupils are alike. One way to overcome this successfully, and achieve results is by keeping in mind last week's lesson.

Do not get into the habit of discarding what was so important a week earlier. Being still in a weak stage, adding new pieces does need more time. Without this process, the new material becomes difficult to handle. I am reminded of one mother telling me: "My daughter was enjoying her lessons so much until her teacher gave her the next book in order, and it was so difficult she lost interest and quit".

Life is great when it is understood. The opposite causes the greatest damage. If not understood properly; what is the point of continuing! Once the blockage occurs it is time to change course. When this happens the pupils drop on the wayside. Some survive, but most do not.

Some teachers feel they must keep pounding the new material, as the parents want to get their monies worth with each lesson. It is not an easy task to accomplish in this position. However, even how unpleasant it seems, some seeds do sprout, so we will leave it at that. Darlings, with that out of the way, let us begin our work.

In the Original Book, which is Volume One, we had the premise that stated the basis of what was to follow. It is important to understand that the beginning is in order. The cover spells out the particulars of this special task.

Volume II follows suit in these harmonious series. After completing the First Book, use it consistently to keep the same principles. Actually, the structure never changes. The problems occur when more knowledge is added at a speed that cannot be obtained. This is where learning should be at a speed that is comfortable.

Do refresh your mind by going over the various aspects of the printed components to clarify, and make it easier to understand. When looking at a new music piece, a pupil is anxious to go at it. The roadblocks appear immediately. What we want is easy access, and smooth sailing. But alas: this in not to be.

Just as the "Health Care of 2010" with over 2000 pages of unread commitments, shows how lax the Congress is in reading the material. Some music students behave in the same manner. A quick look at a piece, and it is expected to be absorbed like magic. Knowledge is acquired through careful inquiry, and awareness that has been grasped by the mind.

By only looking at the material, reason will reveal it does not work. Of course it would be nice if we had the ability, but we were not constructed in that manner. The mind is complicated, but once we learn to understand it, we are rewarded for a lifetime.

It is time to delve into the Minor Scales. A Minor Mode is melancholy (a tendency to be sad,) a powerful influence from the Major Scales: a feeling of great joy, and pleasure. Going from a minor key to a major key shows much emotion of various complex reactions. Much like the change in the weather, one could say extreme, and as far as possible from each other.

THE RELATIVE MINOR SCALE

This Scale is built on the 6th tone of the Major Scale, or a step and a half down, which gives us the same starting point. The Key Signature is the same as the Major Scale. The Relative Minor Scale is also called the Natural Scale in its unaltered form.

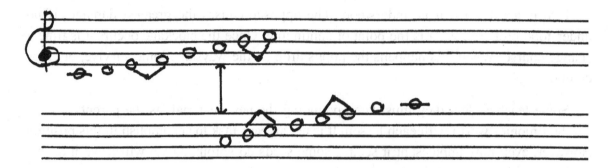

The C Major Scale has the Half Steps between the E-F, and B-C. The Minor Scale: (derived from the C Major Scale) has the same Half Steps in the Natural Mode.

HARMONIC MINOR SCALE

If we raise the 7th tone of the Natural Minor Scale by one half-step we have the Harmonic Minor Scale.

This Harmonic Minor Scale, the one shown above has the same Scale, but notice of the difference in their construction. This Scale contains the tones of the Principal Harmonies of the Minor Keys: the Tonic Chord (I) A-C-E, the Sub-Dominant Chord (IV) D-F-A and the Dominant Chord (V) E-G#-B (play two Octaves and the B will appear).

It is very important to memorize this fact. Of course, it is only a part of the whole to keep in mind. This is like the Stars in the Sky, there is no end, just the beginning Dears.

MELODIC MINOR SCALE

The Natural Minor Scale also gives us the Melodic Minor Scale: This is formed by raising the 6th and 7th tones one half step. However, only in ascending does this take place. While descending the Natural Minor Scale is used. All of this is quite interesting, but difficult to understand.

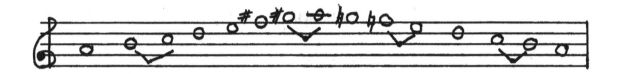

THE FIRST 5 TONES OF ALL THE MINOR MODES ARE THE SAME.
THE ALTERATIONS ARE MADE ON THE 6th AND 7th TONES

Music may be written in many different Modes, or are also called Scales. Most of it has been in the Major, and Minor Modes. The Relative Minor of C Major is A Minor, count 6 up from C, including C, and the 6 upwards is A. We will be using the Harmonic Minor Scale, as this Mode contains the Principle Tones of the Minor Key, and this is: the TONIC CHORD A-C-E ---- SUB-DOMINANT CHORD ---D-F-A--- and the DOMINANT CHORD --- E G# B.

THE NATURAL, HARMONIC, AND MELODIC MINOR SCALES

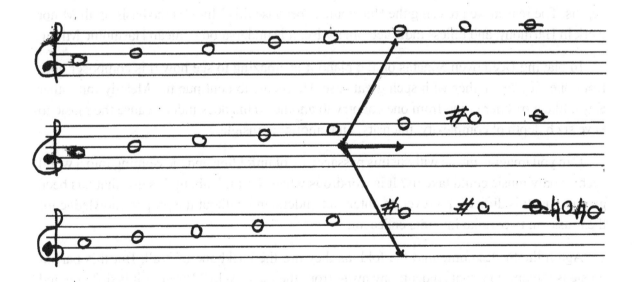

CHAPTER TWO

*****

LESSON 2

MINOR KEYS

Do keep in mind that the 1st 5 tones of the Relative Minor (or also called the Natural Minor Scale) the Harmonic and Melodic start their journey on the same path, but after that they continue in different directions. If this is not clear in the mind, things could get complicated. These three types of Minor Keys have variations in their intervals, which produce contrast with the Major Keys.

It is not unusual for some composers to add all three of the Minor Keys into one piece. I set myself to discover at least one of them, and low and behold I did find one. How about you going about, and find one on your own. With the zillions of songs in this Universe, that should be an interesting journey. In Volume One: the piece called "Greensleeves" is written in the Melodic Mode.

Below, we have the Sharp Scales, and starting on the 6th tone of the Major Scale the Minor begins. The reason we are using the Harmonic is because this Minor is the basis of all Minor work in Harmony, and unless indicated otherwise, it is understood to mean Harmonic Minor.

In playing Beethoven Sonatas on the piano it is amazing to see how this composer goes from one Key to another with such great ease. He seems to continue the Melody into other Keys, like a traveler going from one country to another. This does indeed cause the music to have such depth of complexity, intensity, and emotional insight.

Can you imagine music without this passageway of unfolding and blossoming into a world such as only music could take us? It is wondrous when we think about this gift that has been given to us. It is difficult however, to enter and understand without the proper knowledge for the musician to partake into this endeavor.

Again the Scales come into the fold, as they are the backbone of it all. But this part of music is the one spot that students shy away from the most. Why? Because it is difficult and requires much work. By that I mean a great deal of concentration. It seems to lead in that direction. If you live long enough the truth will bear it out.

HARMONIC MINOR –SHARPS

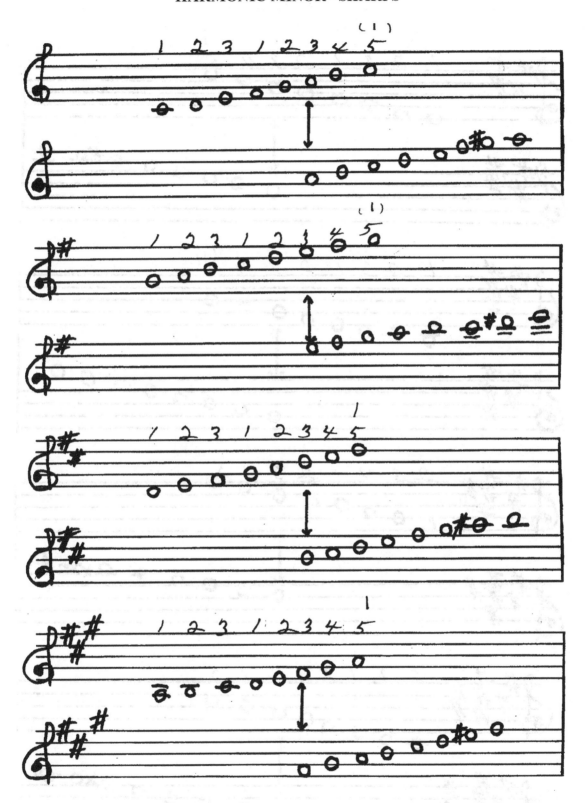

HARMONIC MINOR -SHARPS

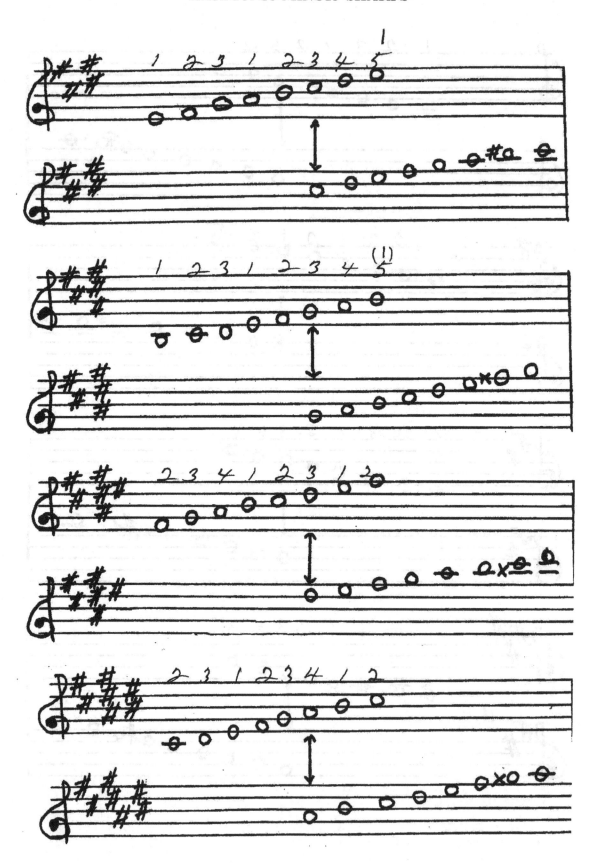

8

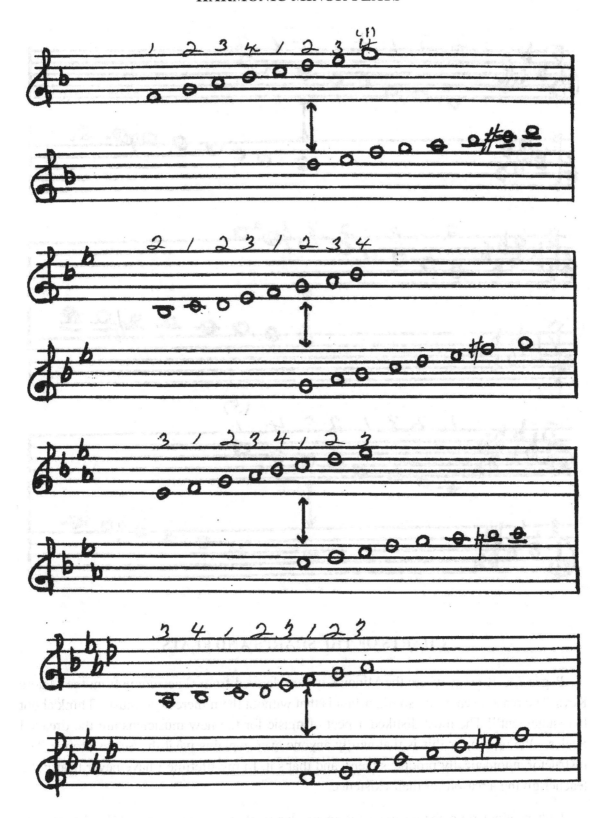

HARMONIC MINOR –FLATS

CHARTS OF THE SHARPS AND FLATS

Pages 7 to 10 show where the Minor Keys are derived from. They come from the Majors Keys. The reason Scales are so important is that without them there is no music. Think about that statement!!! The most disliked aspect of music for the new musicians are the dreaded Scales. One reason for this is that hardly anyone ever explains what the Scales are for. The instructor automatically produces them, and that's it. In my lifetime I have never heard of a teacher giving a reason for their existence.

Isn't it about time for an explanation to clarify this well-kept secret? Scales are the backbone of it all. Although, I heard of one student who played so many scales that there was

10

hardly any time for the pieces to be played. I wonder if the teacher ever told her why she had to play so many that the neighbor next door complained about her practice.

Darlings, at this stage of the game, I am sure your interest is so acute, and extremely great that the instrument of your desire will burst forth in some fashion. Of course, it is important to play the scales when first starting lessons, as they not only help the student with the fingering around the piano keys, or whatever other instrument one is playing. They also exercise the fingers to be agile and help to navigate, and control the fingers as no other can, plus they really find their way around the instrument.

Another thing they do at the same time is to corroborate the mind and fingers to make strong at the same time. This does accelerate the process of instrument playing, and if the student knows what is happening when during the practice, then he is showing superior intellect. On the other hand, if a mindless attitude is put in place, that is what one gets: Nothingness! So, we will leave it at that.

If, no instrument is in sight, then we will continue using our intellectual powers. The amazing thing is that it feels so right. This is because that is where our universe exists. How wondrous the thought. The totality of it all and it is within us to go to the source, and it will give us everything we need. This entry is open for all times, and if there were a charge for it, can you imagine at what cost?

In the world we live in now, it seems even the air is chargeable, but fortunately for us going into our private sacred inner divine entry is for our very own passage. That is something to be thankful for. To get back to earth, isn't it discouraging when moving along smoothly to suddenly come to an impasse: where there is no outlet? What to do? I'm afraid not much Dears. It goes to show there is a lot of poor material out there.

The music business is out to make money. The information that is given is very sparse. Some books seem to make a simple explanation impossible to understand. When I took some Drum Lessons in Manhattan in my time, the instructor who had his studio on the 2nd floor of the building, played in a band in New Jersey, and said to me: "By the time we are finished, and I drive home it is 3:a.m. I arrive here at 7:a.m. I never get more than 3 hours of sleep.

While he listens to me play with the Drum Sticks, he is busy packing boxes, moving around here and there. When he finally sits down near the end of the lesson he is putting the finishing touches to a new music book he is writing. He explains: "I just copy the rhythm section from this here clarinet book, and use it for my drum book." I taught, "What a cheat!!!"

His interest was in producing as many books as possible, as he forced the finished product on his students. I have seen so many students fall on the wayside where the instructions fizzle into a maze. The same is true from the T.V. guitars lessons. The pupil ends up buying an expensive instrument with steel strings, and gets bloody fingers from his efforts. I wonder how many fall for this scheme. It does disturb me to see this happen, but it is not the fault of the student.

CHAPTER THREE

*****

LESSON 3

MUSIC IN THE MINOR KEY

Since we have all this information about Music in the Minor Keys, it is time to introduce a piece of music that is in the Minor Mode. You will notice immediately the stark contrast between the Minor and Major Keys. The Minor is really melancholy and is crying for some release from this sadness of life. When it does go into the Major all is well and happy. But isn't what this Life is all about, and the Music of these Modes joins with us. It seems to go hand in hand with it all.

It is true we do not have G# in the Key of D Minor. Page 13, the piece (Marche Slav) what we do have is D-E-F-G-A-Bb-C#-D. This is where we must tread with caution. Where did this G# come from? This mystery must be solved. Where do we begin? The piece starts with 5 notes coming downward. Take careful notice of the G# being right next to the A note! Isn't it strange that the 5th tone of the D minor scale happens to be A, and in the A minor Scale the 7th degree called the Leading Tone happens to be a G# leading right into the A, to complete the Scale.

In measure 6 a C# appears right next to the D, which in the Major Mode has a C#: thus D-E-F#-G-A-B-C#-D. But in the Minor Mode it also has a C#: D-E-F- G-A Bb-C#-D. As you may recall D Minor comes from the F Major Scale, and Dears, this Scale has a Bb in it plus the C#. Playing the Melody in the mind and taking the interest to watch each step along the way will make it clear that we could use this information in Transposing into another Key for our future development.

To accomplish this: Form a D Minor Chord in your mind, and hold it for as long as need be: D-F-A. When you feel up to going ahead take the next step and start the Melody. Play the 5th finger on the A, and hold it for the count of 1-2, then the 4th finger on the G# for the next beat and then roll down the hill with the rest of the fingers for the 4th beat, and it brings us into the next measure.

Jumping into measure 6, notice that we are landing into C# and this can caused a problem in understanding the How and Why of it all. However, because a D Minor Scale, having a C# as the leading 7th tone (D-E-F-G-A-Bb C# D) into the Tonic D, accounts for it.

MARCHE SLAV

PIANO VERSION
Three Chords--- D minor---D-F-A---G minor---G-Bb-D---A Major A-C#-E

MARCHE SLAV

GUITAR VERSION
MUSIC - (PETER ILYICH TCHAIKOVSKY) RUSSIAN COMPOSER (1840-1893)
The above show 3 basic chords, and 3 Bar Chords

14

THE HAPPY FARMER

PIANO VERSION

Four Chords ---F Major---Bb Major---G7 ---C major

15

GUITAR CHORDS P. 18
MUSIC BY ROBERT ALEXANDER SCHUMANN (1810-1856).

The Basic Chords and the Bar Chords will be explained as we go along. The Bar Chords are quite complex to understand at the beginning. Remember, we are dealing with only the 1st 7 letters of the Alphabet. These are repeated in a zillion ways, and we must keep this in mind. The trick is to improve our thinking, and keep things in order, or it will go haywire.

A little bit each day, and the progress will be noticed as we skip along the path. This is how the learning process speeds ahead, like learning a new language. Of course, a child does this automatically, without the need of a printed body of words. It just goes to show that adults do have a trying time adding another language to their repertoire. The difference being that a child has more time to assimilate than has the adult.

As adults, we do carry along much that could be eliminated, if that is the case then some things could be made free to put in the time for our music. It all comes down to make room for what needs to be done. This time could then be used for some real results. Time is of the essence. In Life we do make space without realizing it when the mood strikes. If that fizzles out, then something else will take its place in short order. Only the deep-seated desires take root, and we move along with it.

The Minor Mode, as compared to the Major Mode, does indeed have powerful emotions that intermingle with the human mind. Since the mind reasons, thinks, feels, perceives, judges etc., music certainly plays a great part of each day of our lives. I wonder how much time is devoted to this one aspect. Can we live without it? I think not.

It is a wonderful addition added unto us. Of course each one of us has our very own special preference. It does give us pleasure when listening to music, The hours that are second nature to a being is done unconsciously for most of the day. But it is there! At some point in the day we may stop and listen for a few minutes, and then go back to what we were doing.

So, it is difficult in a normal day to devote our undivided attention, unless of course a concert is attended, and money is spent, then it is felt that we stay put, and give it our all. However, on a daily basis it is a different matter. The music is on for most of the day, but it becomes background music. We become so accustomed that a void is felt if silence occurs.

This is true in movie making: What would it be like without the background music? Have you ever thought about it? Once you eliminate the music in movie making, everything goes flat, and stays that way until the music is slowly brought in. It just feels so natural for this background to be in place.

Once it has been realized that Music is indeed necessary to our well-being, then we could skip along with a purpose in this respect, and this then brings us back to the topic at hand. In learning new material in just about anything, the interest must be there, and depending on how much of it exists will then decide the outcome. However, since this point has been reached, I believe we are on our way Darlings.

So let's not waste any more time. A little each day really goes a very long way. Even with a small bit of knowledge of music lessons, it is great fun to grab an easy book that may have been played at earlier times, and just sight-read it again. You can judge your progress in this manner. Each time a piece is played for light entertainment in this fashion it is amazing to see how much ahead we have come by. Also, try to read some music that is brand new, but not difficult, and just play for the enjoyment of it.

There is no joy in just plowing away, and waiting for a miracle to happen, and dreaming we could play with a flourish. But by actually doing it with the easier pieces comes to the same end however we reach it in various stages of progress. We may never reach the stage we are dreaming about, and let's face it, may not live long enough for it to happen. The goal is to enjoy the breaks as we move with it, and not to wait for the impossible.

CHORDS FOR THE PIECE

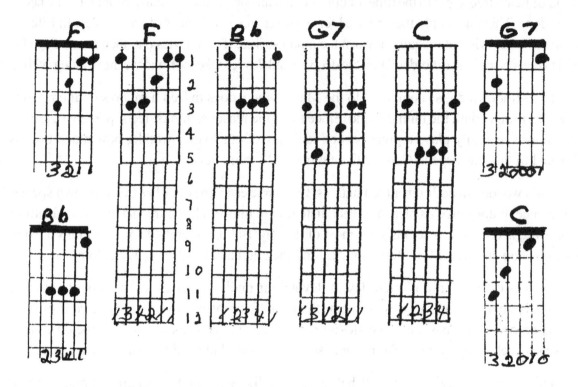

As you notice the Chart has the regular Chords, and also the corresponding Bar Chords. So, you have a choice, and when practicing, play the Basic one and then to cement to mind play the Bar Chords. Start slowly and analyze the Chords as you go along, starting with the F Chord. Notice that they look alike, expect for the fact that the Bar has an extra note. The fifth string is added, which happens to be C, and is part of the F. So, why is this different?

If the Bar played the 5th string on the 1st fret it would read as a Bb, and the F Chord does not have a Bb. This may not be earth shattering news to a non-musician, but to a Guitar Player it happens to be. Now that that has been resolved, let us go to the next one, which is the Bb Chord. This is another instance of both Chords looking alike. What is the difference?

This time the Bar does need the 5th strings 1st fret Bb. Because being a movable Chord, it cannot be like the regular Chord. In a non-movable the 5th string reads as an open A. The Bb does not have an A in it. However, it does indeed have an A if used as a Bb7 Chord. But we are dealing with a Chord with 3 notes, not a 7th. If we tried to use the Basic Bb Chord as a movable one, it would not work.

Because moving it up one fret would then read F#-D# B-F#, or to put it into order, (B-D# F#-2nd fret) The Bar however acts properly by adding the Bb on the 5th string A of the 1st fret. To go further with this: If moved up the ladder to the next fret, would give a C Chord, (3rd fret) reading C- G-C-E-G and continuing along in this fashion you would come to the conclusion that the open A would always be just that. Open A, and would follow until through the very end.

18

Do a little each day, without realizing it the brain does pick it up. It becomes something familiar as parts are added onto it. Anything new does not seem to register immediately; it needs more time to assimilate.

The G7 Chords look very different from one another. The long grid has the Bar Chord. It reads as: 1st string on the 3rd fret is a G—2nd is D—3rd on the 4th fret is B, and the 4th string on the 3rd fret is F, and the 5th string is D, and the 6th string on the 3rd fret is G. This adds up to G, B, D, F, with the G and D repeated. This gives us 6 notes of the G7th Chord.

The Basic Chord reads as: 1st string 1st fret is F. 2, 3, and 4 are all open strings as follows: Open B, G, and D. The 5th string 2nd fret is B, and the 6th string 3rd fret is G. This reads as a G7 Basic Chord. G, B, D, G, B, F. "Reading from the 6th string to the 1st".

The C Bar Chord reads as follows: 1st string 3rd fret is G. The 2nd 3rd and 4th string reads as: E, C, G. The 5th string on the 3rd fret is C. The Basic Chord of C is as follows: The 1st string is open E. The 2nd string on the 1st fret is C. The 3rd string is open G. The 4th string on the 2nd fret is E, and the 5th string on the 3rd fret is C. Only 5 strings are played Dears.

Commit the Chords to memory. This is a good start for the use of the Bar Chords, sort of to get acquainted with them. On page 20 of the Quick Reference Chart it has the Basic Chords. When sitting in a Subway Train, a good way to pass the time, and put it to good use is to mentally go over the Chords. It is amazing no matter how many times one goes over something like this, it is never boring because the brain can't get enough of it.

The problem begins when the lapse of time is too great, and all good intentions are non-existent. Even bad habits are kept alive, because they are repeated many times over. So, if you want this to happen with your music, do not follow this example.

When going over the Quick Reference Chart, and if you should happen to be waiting for a Plane to take you wherever, and you have a long wait the time could fly faster than your trip. Use different starting points. On this particular trip, go over the puzzle of how Scales add #'s or Flat's as they move around. Let us take the Key of C. Why does it not have any at all? The answer: Because remembering way back in Volume 1. The pattern was given and it showed that the Major Scale of C, the model, had a set pattern. Once this pattern was followed, all of the Major Scales then would have the same pattern.

Now, this is how it all started. The Pattern is simple. Without it one just has a maze like groping in the dark. Learning can be a pleasure when doing it properly. However, the opposite is true, and can become a nightmare. Knowing the information is accurate and observing each detail, then put it in your memory bank for safe keeping.

Don't be a grasshopper. Stay put, and let it seep in. Of course with the zillions of information about every conceivable subject in this universe, we can't be hogs, but must be polite and choose carefully what are needs are, Darlings.

QUICK REFERENCE OF GUITAR CHORDS

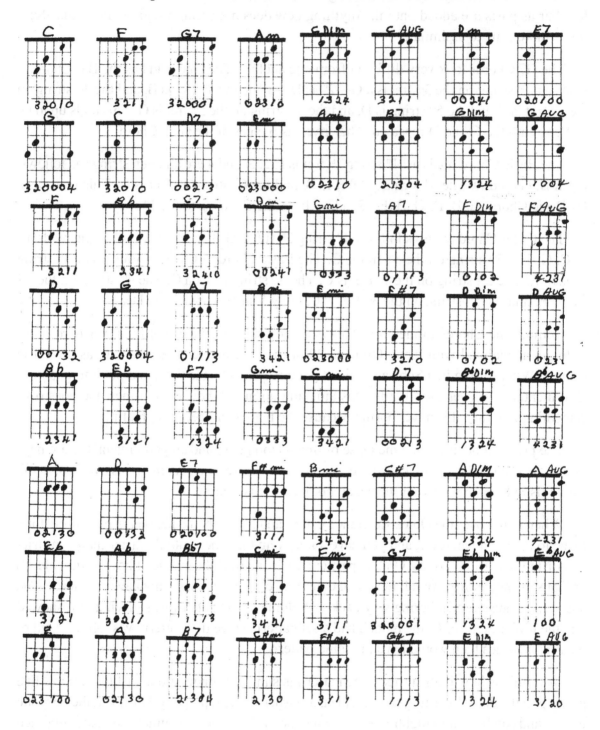

CHAPTER FOUR

*****

LESSON 4

TRANSPOSING

Transposing is to reproduce in a different key, by raising or lowering its pitch, to perform a piece of music in a key other than the one which it is written. For an example: The song called Long, Long Ago seems like a simple piece, and also being in the Key of C. It has no #'s or flats, and having only 2 chords: C and G7. In trying to understand something that is complicated as we move along. I believe the simple way is the best to go about it. Also, it is more interesting to solving problems, if it is being absorbed along the journey.

Looking carefully at the starting point of the original piece, take notice that the piece starts with a half note of 2 counts, and then 2 quarter notes that equal the 4 counts that fill the measure. The next two measures have the exact counting, but on the fourth measure it has a whole count of the entire four beats.

The second line is a bit different. It starts out with the half note, and the two quarter notes, but the next measure has a whole note of four counts. The next two measures repeat themselves. Before we go further, go back to the beginning, and notice that these two lines of melody have their little song of 8 measures.

The following 8 measures are exact duplicates, except for the very last one. Instead of having a whole note, like the other measures it has a dotted half note of 3 beats, and a quarter rest of one beat, which comes to 4 beats. The melody also is a repeat. With all of this information, it does mean that the piece written for 4 beats to a measure is all set to move along.

VERSE
Tell - me the tales- that to me – were so dear- - -
Long- long a go - - - Long - long a go - - -
Sing – me the songs– I de light - ed to hear - - -
Long – long a go - - - long – long a go - - -

The Verse now is set to music in the Key of G on the next page. After committing it to memory, sing the song to the music. How perfectly it all works out. It seems so simple, so why bother. But, the understanding of it is what is important. For this evolves in music of long standing. It shows how composers create out of seemingly nothing into something of worth.

LONG, LONG, AGO

FINGERING
Same as Key of C

23

LONG, LONG, AGO

FINGERING
1-----1—2—3-----3—1—4-----5—4--2--------
5-----4—3—2--------4----3—2—1--------Repeat--

24

LONG, LONG, AGO

FINGERING
Same as Key of D

LONG, LONG, AGO

FINGERING
Same as Key of D

26

LONG, LONG, AGO

FINGERING

1----1—2—3----3—1—4—5—4—2-----
3-----1—3—2----------4----3—2—1--------

LONG, LONG, AGO

FINGERING

2-----2—3--4-----3--1--4-----5--4—2----------
5-----4—3—2--------4-----3—2—1--------

LONG, LONG, AGO

FINGERING

2-----2—3—1-----1—2—3-----4—3—1--------
3-----2—1—2----------3-----1—3—2--------

EXPLANATION

The 7 versions of Long, Long, Ago (after the original C) is to show how the same piece can be Transposed into others Keys. The song in not altered from the Original, the pattern is the same, but it is just in other Keys. There are times when certain instruments and also human voices need to be placed in a higher or lower position. It would be a drawback to keep the piece only in the Original Key, and never move from that again.

Do notice that the Key of C has the C and the G7 Chord. For the Guitarist this is a good workout in trying out the Bar Chords. Count 5 from C, C-D-E-F-G, this brings us to the 5th degree of the Scale, but with an added 7th, which then makes it a G 7th Chord.

We live in a very orderly world: "Nothing by chance, Darlings." Follow the rules and you can't go wrong. Mess up the rules, and go into a tail spin. To stay on the top of it is the way to go. Composers who go into new directions, and try out other forms: which is never ending, could only do so if they understand the rules first, so as to break them into new ventures. This can be done into new styles of music, but with the backing of what it is all about.

Going into the Centuries when music started to be written down, then as more knowledge was added on and grew into a colossal ocean of music. Rules can be broken, but only if it is understood first. The basic form must be intact, like building a house, it must have structure: then the designer could go wild and built a Sky Scrapper. But all in all it must be some form of a house.

"Key of D" has the Chords D and A7. The reason the 7th was added on is because the original pattern had a 7th, so by going into the other Keys we must keep the pattern intact. Now we have another piece of baggage added on to the 1st sharp, which was F# and now a C #. These two #'s make up the D Scale.

The Key of A now has 3#'s. We keep the last 2#'s, and must now add the 3rd #. But you might ask, "Where are they coming from? They are added on in 5th's. They are not haphazardly put together. If the core is correct, and each new # is properly placed, then we are in the right direction. Life also is run in that order, although many times, we do not realize it.

The journey continues, as our train having these important stops to add our #'s. The 4th # comes along with the Key of E. Keep all of the previous #', but now add the 4th #. Try to figure out the name of the new #. The next Key in order is the Key of B. This one has 5#'s. The added new # emerges, and see if you could name it. I realize that our baggage has added on more than we could carry. So, let us take a break and stop in a Diner, and have some lunch, and mull this over. We have some confusion here with the added #'s and the Chords. It is true that the Key Signature has the #'s added on in 5th's but be careful here, because the Chords are also added on in 5th's. We are working on the Chords, which are the same for the Guitar and the Piano. No difference Dears.

The Key Signature in C has no #'s or flats. Starting with the next in order, counting 5 from C gives us G, with our first #, an F. The next is the Key of D, and how did we come to that? Again counting 5 from the last Key, the D appears, this time with two #'s. Be careful, as we have to account for the two #'s, and where they came from. Well, since the last Key had only one #, keep in mind what that # was called.

Very important: Yes, it was F#, we never lose fact that we must carry this first # forever Dears, as long as it is in the Key of G. This continues into the Key of D, but with the added # of C. When we enter the next Key it is called A, which has 3 #. First there was the F#, then C# and now the new # is G#. Notice these #'s are coming on in 5th's. This does not change as they go with the proper order.

Now our train is back on track, and going in the right direction, which is great. Have you ever caught a train, and then realized after a while something was not right? There is no escape, but to go back and restart from the beginning. All the time lost going where it was not suppose too, but someplace else where it was not intended. It is best to know where the train is headed.

Now we could relax, because it is clear sailing. The next stop is the Key of E. All of the other #'s are accounted for, so the next in order is D#. Of course this occurred from the last #, which was G. Keeping this in mind the 5th above the last one is the D#. We could feel happy because all of the #'s are with us.

The Key is B, still going in 5th's, and the next # from the last one is A. This comes to 5 #'s. Repeat in your mind of this state of affairs, and start from the beginning and think: F#, C# G# D#, and now A#.

Hop into the next Key from the B that we just left, still going in 5th's and this is called Key of F#. Our baggage is really getting heavy, in more ways than one. Now the problem is: Why do we have a Key called F#, when we already had an F# in the Key of G? The answer to that is because that F# belongs to that Key. This F# came from the order of 5$^{th's.}$ The 5th degree from the Scale of B to the next in order is F#. Now there are 6 #'s. F#, C#, G#, D#, A#, and E#. This E# is called enharmonic, meaning that it lands on F/E#; this is still in perfect order.

After the Key of F# we have the Key of C#. This one is a heavy one as it has 7 #'s. Let's repeat again all of the #'s in this Scale, all 7 of them. The 1st one which was F#, then continue, C#, G#, D#, A#, E#, and B#. Notice that the B# falls on C. Again, this is an enharmonic change. Our trip has come a long way from where we started. So, Darlings lets share our joy in accomplishing this Good Work.

****

CHAPTER FIVE

*****

LESSON 5

STEPHEN FOSTER COLLINS

Was one of America's best-loved songwriters. He had little musical training, but he had a great gift of melody. At the age of 6, he taught himself to play the clarinet. He composed "The Tioga Waltz" for piano at 14 years of age. Two years later his first song, "Open thy Lattice, Love" was published.

He settled in Pittsburgh to work as a composer. Some of Foster's songs became so popular during his lifetime that they were adapted (with suitable words) for Sunday school use.

The composer Charles Ives often quoted Foster's tunes in his music when he wanted a real American flavor. Morton Gould's "A Foster Gallery" for orchestra is another example of the appeal of the songs. Because they are deeply rooted in America folk traditions, the best of Foster's songs have become part of the American cultural heritage.

He wrote "Oh! Susanna" in 1846. It became the favorite of the "forty-niners" in the California gold rush. News of the gold discovery spread quickly, and thousands of persons rushed to establish gold claims. These "forty-niners," as they were called poured from all parts of the world. Some who were not so lucky in the gold fields became farmers or ranchers. But, "Oh! Susanna" lives on regardless of gold or not.

Songs can be divided into two groups, some by composers we know, or those by unknown origin. No one really knows who composed the beautiful English folk song called "Greensleeves." Songs can be divided into either Popular, or Art songs. Hundreds, or should I say by the "ship-load" of popular songs fade away, never to be heard again despite their popularity during their hey-day. There is a good reason for songs that last forever, for they leave an impression that is never forgotten.

MY OLD KENTUCKY HOME

Stephen Collins Foster (1826-1864)

Born in Lawrenceville, Pennsylvania on July 4th, 1826
Song was written and set to music by Stephen Collins Foster in 1850, and published in 1853, It was designated the "State Song of Kentucky" by an act of Legislature (Kentucky Acts, 1928) Approved March 19, 1928.

It was not until 1924 that "My Old Kentucky Home" became associated with Kentucky's main event: The Kentucky Derby- Original Title in 1850 "Poor Uncle Tom, Goodnight" Publisher's Title in 1853 "My Old Kentucky Home." The Original lyrics were written in 1853. The Contemporary Lyrics written in 1986, and revised by House Resolution 159.

Foster began to compose at the age of 16. His name soon became recognized. One of his earlier songs, which swept the country, was the popular "Oh, Susanna." He wrote more than 200 songs during the next fifteen years and beyond. Few are scarcely known today, however, one remains an all favorite today, "Beautiful Dreamer" written in 1862, and published in 1864, after his death. He is buried in Pennsylvania.

MY OLD KENTUCKY HOME

```
     ##
    # G    |A |   |A    |    |D   |   |A  |
          THE |SUN SHINES bRIGHT in the |OLD KEN-TUCK-Y HOME, Tis

    A |    |A    |    |E7 |   |  |A   |   |A   |
    SUM-MER, THE PEOPLE ARE|GAY. THE |CORN-TOPS RIPE AND THE

    D     |    |A   |    |A   |    |D   |   |
    MEAD-OWS IN THE bLOOM, WHILE THE |bIRDS MAKE MUS-IC ALL THE

    A ||   |   |A   |   |   |   |D   |   |  |
    DAY   THE|YOUNG FOLKS ROLL ON THE|LIT-TLE CA-bIN FLOOR, ALL

    A    |   |A   |   |E7 |   |   |A  |   |   |   |
    MER-RY ALL HAPPY AND|bRIGHT  BY'N bY|EH HARD TIMES COME a

    D     |   |A   |   |  |A    |   |E7 |  |A || ξ |
    KNOCK ING AT THE DOOR, THEN MY|OLD KEN-TUCK-Y HOME GOOD NIGHT!

    A |   |D   |  |A   ||B7 D|   ||   |A ||  |
    WEEP NO MORE MY|LA-DY  OH WEEP NO MORE TO-DAY!   WE WILL

    A  |   |   |   |D   |   |A  |   |
    SING ONE SONG FOR MY|OLD KEN-TUCK-Y HOME FOR  THE

    A    |   |E7   |   |A || ξ  ||
    OLD KEN-TUCY-Y HOME FAR a-|WAY.
```

GUITAR CHORDS

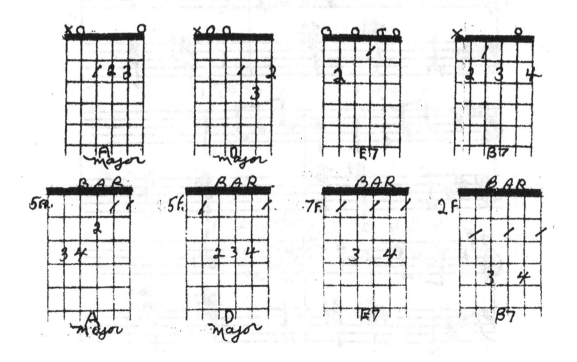

35

BEAUTIFUL DREAMER

BEAUTIFUL DREAMER

EXPLANATION

Both of the Foster Songs would be in realm of the studies of the first two Books. It is nice to be able to play these pieces without too much ado. The only problem would be the Bar Chords. However, this is optional, so, Darlings enjoy the music.

If you have some Music Books from your past lessons, and they are in the early stages, drag them out and play like a pro. We must stop now and then as we climb the mountain, not only to refresh ourselves and to savor all the hard work that was put into our studies.

Remember, all work and no play is not the way to go. As the upward climb is ceaseless, it is like working all day without stopping for some nourishment. Know your limitations. Many students push too hard, and end up with nothing. Just do what must be done with a clear mind of where you are heading, and most importantly, enjoy what you set out to do.

The world has much to offer, and the older one gets, we do learn not to put too much on the plate. We must be selective, or the crush of an avalanche will overwhelm us to call it quits. So, Dears, do only what is comfortable, as too much in a 24 hr. day in not good, so do keep that in mind.

BEAUTIFUL DREAMER

D BEAU-TI-FUL DREAM-ER, | G WAKE UN-TO me,

A7 STAR-LighT AND DEW-DROPS ARE WAiTING FOR | D ThEE

D SOUNDS OF THE RUDE WORLD | G hEARD IN ThE DAY,

A7 LUll'D BY ThE mOONLighThAVE ALL PASSED A-

D WAY! | A7 BEAU-Ti-FUL DREAm-ER,

D QUEEN OF my SONG, | E7 LiST WhiLE I WOO ThEE WiTh

SOFT MEL-O-DY A7 | D GONE ARE ThE CARES OF

G LiFE'S BUSY ThRONG, | A7 BEAUTIFUL DREAMER A-WAKE UNTO

D mE! | A7 BEAU-Ti-FUL DREAmER A WAKE ON TO | D mE!

CHORDS

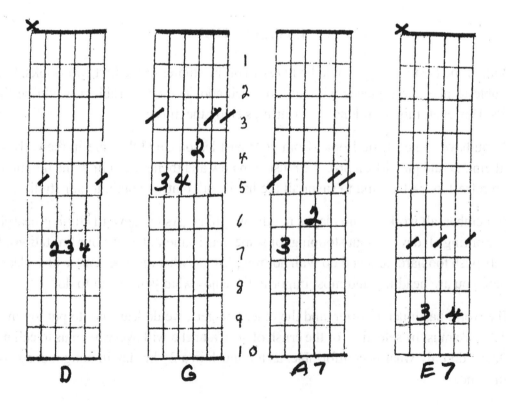

D   G   A7   E7

REVIEW OF THE WORK SO FAR

It is a good idea to clear our mind of what has been presented. Let us stop and absorb what has been gained from this knowledge. Adding too much, and not giving it enough time to become part of our lives, could become lost in the vast desert of time. To become cultivated and well nourished, as with feeding the body, the mind also needs the same attention. If too much space is left with not understanding where we are going with it, then the mind will fill up the space with nonsense that was not asked for.

In the learning process we must keep a tight grip on what we want, or it will slip away right in front of our eyes. This is so true as to be unbelievable. I suppose this was intentional. Otherwise every time we step outside the door all of the sights and sounds would automatically fill the brain and clog our thinking catastrophically. Do we need to go any further with this thought?

The Great Thinkers of the past spent time on this subject. The greatest flaw is in not having a clear passageway along the route. It is indeed wonderful to experience this trip. We can make it so at this moment with our Music. All the energy that was put into this venture so far was well worth the effort. However, how much was actually retained is the real test. Let us go back and see how far the progression worked.

A second go at it is a real teaser. The first time around all was new and exciting, and a thrill to behold, but how much did stick is the Question. It may seem boring to read it all over again. Parts of it may be skipped over, but the juice of it most likely needs special attention. Going over a Scale, especially one with the 7 Sharps will occupy your time, as a starter Dears.

At first glance it is interesting to look at it and turn the page to the next item. However, the second time around we could give it a mean look, and ponder if we should continue or try to pry it open. I would venture to say take the latter choice. If it seems impossible, then keep the page open, and just look it over, without doing anything. But be surprised as you do this it will become more familiar if a steady flow of this treatment follows.

Have a set time of the day for your studies, just as is done for our daily meals and the rest of what makes a day in our lives. Just make sure the Music is not left out of this time that we do without thinking Darlings, because it seems to be automatic. Put it on the fast tract, and before you know it, the Music is not a chore anymore, but something pleasant to behold, because, it becomes part of us.

Once this happens, it is not a new subject to tackle every day, and then get annoyed by the interference. It becomes something we want to do, and look forward to its appearance. This then is what we are looking for, and accept it in our lives. Now, Darlings, let us go on with our MUSIC.

CHAPTER SIX

*****

LESSON 6

STYLE

To make a simple piece more interesting, and knowing the scales does help tremendously to play folk music with style. If a piece is written in the Key of C, and has just the regular notes with chords, one could play an opening at the beginning as an introduction. Knowing the scales is a must, for it opens up the avenue, not only for understanding what one is doing, but also has a wealth of material for doing it.

Taking a chord and playing it in a broken form, gives a pleasant sound. When starting with the left hand, form the chord, and instead of playing it solid, play each note separately. After the left hand plays the three notes, then switch over to the right hand, and continue this process, and finish the cycle with the left hand, using only the one note of the root of the chord to complete the form.

These broken chords are called Arpeggios. Playing just one octave gives a complete sound. However, not stopping there, but moving upwards, and reaching a few octaves. Since the Arpeggio was started with the left hand, then to put a close to the passage it will be done with the left hand. This time the second finger will be used to end the flow. The opening is complete, and the piece can be started, Darlings.

A good idea may be to go into the different keys to establish in the mind to make this as fluid as possible, and at the same time learn the arpeggios and put them to good use. By using the keys in as many ways as possible, and not just as an exercise, does indeed make the practice worthwhile.

Can you imagine how well the composers of the past who have created such great works, could have accomplished their great music without knowing the scales. I wonder how many musicians realize the depth of this statement. Of course knowing the scales with its finer points is no easy task. That is why great composers, especially like one of the greatest: BACH: About 60 to 70 Bach's are known to have been musicians. Johann Sebastian Bach is considered the "greatest genius of baroque music." We will find out more about him as we go along.

HOME ON THE RANGE

We are adding a little flourish to this piece, as we are at a stage where a little spice will help to make it more interesting Dears. Chopin's music is very delicate, and his style has a great deal of freedom that makes it sound different. Have you noticed through the years that many pianists who have a style and play perhaps in clubs that do use this embellishment? You also may be familiar with this fanciful ornament, and it certainly makes a difference to highlight a piece.

This could be used in other pieces. So, we will take the piece in another key and add this same ornamental stroke into our memory. Only from practice does it become a natural process to make a piece interesting. Of course this applies to songs where we have the freedom to do so, or if composing our own music, as we can't change Classical Music, or other Standard music that is set in stone.

HOME ON THE RANGE

A HOME ON THE RANGE

A HOME ON THE RANGE

We have different versions of this song starting on p.41, which is in the Key of G. First know what Key the Piece is in. Look carefully, and see it is the Key of G, which has 1 #, and that is F#. Also the Time Signature is ¾. It starts with the G Chord, split up with a Bass note of G, and then 2 solid G Chord, which completes the measures. This goes along happily for 5 measures with the Chords of G, C and then an A on measure 6. The 7th and 8th turns into a broken D Chord called an arpeggio.

This D Chord comes from the Key of G, found on the 5th degree of the Scale: GA B C D E F# G. Then it continues as before, until it comes to the end of the piece. At this point the Root of the Chord is played, which is the G Chord and final resting place of the piece again in arpeggio form.

The same piece is played again, but in the Key of F. This has been transposed from the G version. However, this one in F is a bit longer. The Chords used are: F-Bb-G-C. Notice that the Chords in the first version have the same pattern as the 2nd one - G-C –A-D.

Starting from the Root of the Chord, both have a 4th distance from each other. Keeping the Root in mind to continue this thinking a 2nd (Root to G) and then a 5th occurs. (Root to C) There are many ways one could go about this and examine the parts, and how to better understand. It is better to dig in and find out how it all works, Darlings.

44

The Key of F has one flat, Bb. It is an exact reproduction of the same piece that was in the Key G, which has one # and is an F#. Now, this may seem confusing, but Darlings if we don't bring it to life at some point of our musical studies how can we progress in a timely manner. We could go further with this and play the piece in all the keys, but I don't think that is necessary, as it is time consuming, and it could be done in a flash if done mentally. This is one reason why it is important to use our mental state of mind.

We do not have to travel with any luggage, so it is easy to accomplish in that respect. However, to keep other thoughts from invading our mission is the challenge. The answer to that is to do little each day, as it is difficult to keep this channel open for any length of time. As soon as we start, the flood gates open, with everything but what is called for. A little does go a long way, and it is more enjoyable if this route is taken.

A feeling of moving along is felt, until the next day, when we continue where we left off. The process does work as it keeps adding to each day in solving problems. Some advancements take more time, and I am speaking of real time like months to understand, but, let's face it, the time will go by with or without us. So, let us travel with it.

The crushing of rushing to get ahead before its time is deadly in more ways than one. Music is more like being in another realm. It is worth the effort to add to our well- being. A little at a time will do it Dears. Just by knowing that we could get away with it because only a few minutes are given to it. The real crunch comes when thinking about this ordeal. When things get difficult, clip some of the over hangings off, and do only a bit at a time.

With most people the thing to do is to train oneself to be on a certain schedule: Since we are individuals we have to find our own set of rules. The trouble starts when we suddenly try to escape from the set pattern. If this happens: KEEP FIRM, and don't give in. At this set back, think of how you will feel if you break your resolve. So, what to do! Be nice and gentle with yourself. And, at great sacrifice give just 5 minutes to the task, and the next day make up for it, and return back on track.

A feeling of great relief will cruise your body as you feel guilt free from the day before. As you continue you should feel much stronger from your ordeal. What this is all about is to impress upon you on how to go ahead when the need is strong to really stick to it. At times another problem will appear to turn you against your wishes. Isn't it amazing how hard we must work against these annoying actions?

It is like a disease that awakens once our electrical impulses come to life. It seems all things imaginable vie for our attention all at once to make sure each one is in first place. Only the strongest will gain access, if we let it happen. The music at this time is foremost, so the others will be kept out at bay. Even with all this chaos, life keeps us on our toes, and of course keeps us hopping. Rightly so, as anything less would put us to sleep Darlings.

"IT HAS BEEN SAID. THERE IS ONLY ONE CHORD IN THE WORLD, IT IS THE COMMON TRIAD. EVERYTHING ELSE IS BUT ADDITIONS TO THIS."

After the Scale of 6#'s is a C#, and that has7#'s. We follow the same order thus: F#-C#-G#-D#-A#-E#-B#. Remember that E# and B# are enharmonic. The E# lands on F. The B# ends up on C. Enharmonic Scales are written differently, but keep in mind the sound is the same. If E# is played and one can see that it is the same as playing F. See if you can find this Scale in one of the other books in this Series. That will give more practice in forging ahead, as spending more time on something other on the subject will give it more cement.

IMPROVISING AN INTRODUCTION

The Dominant of the Key of C is G, and the Key of C is used as
a closing for a final resting place in a piece of music.

INTRODUCTION

In the Key of G, again the Dominant is used, which is a 5th above the root of the Key, and this is the D Chord.

48

In understanding the "Improvising the Introduction" is to look at it carefully, and notice that the C Major Chord climbs up the hill. It starts out by playing a low C with the Left Hand. If the pedal is used on the Piano, keep it down for the whole two measures. Next- A Solid Chord: First with the left hand and then changing to the right hand.

After that we cross the left hand over the right hand to continue to play the next chord. Now this frees the right hand to play the next chord, and we end by crossing over the left hand, but only playing one note: The High C. Take the foot off the pedal at this time as you pop off the finger on the high C with a flourish. By that I mean like a pro over the head, Dears.

Play the solid Chords until they become familiar, then, play them arpeggio style (notes of a chord that are played one after another.) Now all the solid Chords are played in this broken style. This does give a piece of music a nice introduction to what is going to be played. Of course, Classical Music does not need this extra push, as it is complete in itself. With Folk Songs and Popular Music there is much to be desired, as they are sold without a bit of imagination added to them, just plain notes and leave it at that.

If in the Key of C, practice the C Chord in this fashion, if you are interested in the improvising. This will highlight what is to come. It is an introduction to the music, and if you have other pieces, and want to try this arrangement, it would have to be transposed, if it is in another Key. This is one reason why transposition is so important. A piece of music can be played in any key if one has the perseverance, of course anything is quite possible, but the drawback is the saying: **Time is of the essence**.

Our time is limited on just about any subject, and the Universe offers us trillions of things we can do. There is no shortage. Actually it is more than the mind can comprehend, so it is important to know where our limits are. Be selective and narrow down added things that are not needed. When you realize at the start of a day, if there are no appointments, and one is free to do whatever, we can go a little wild.

The feel of freedom is so intoxicating that we can spend the whole day thinking about what to do with this wonderful problem, and before we know it the day is gone. It seems everything is but a moment long. Time moves along as on a journey, and it moves relentlessly, waits for no one: it is up to us to use it wisely.

Hop on board, and take the ride; when thinking about this it is such a gift, and it doesn't cost anything. Rich or poor it is for all. So, the motto of the story is: pick with care when dealing with time. The most time we have is in retirement. The hectic earlier life when younger is filled with responsibility in finding our way. It just proves that it is important to savor, and use it with great thought.

Now, Darlings let us get to work with a feeling of worthiness, and pep up our spirits with this feeling. We must talk to ourselves now and then to get in touch with the fast moving world.

CHAPTER SEVEN

*****

LESSON 7

STRUCTURE OF THE E BAR CHORDS

The open E Chord has its name based on the 6th open E string. The root of the shape is on the 6th string. The bottom support of anything, and in this case it is the root of the Chord, so if you play the E Chord, and move up one fret and bar across the 1st fret, a new Chord is born with a new name, and that is now called an F BAR Chord. It is truly amazing how this actually works.

When the 1st finger presses down all of the 6 strings, it is really replacing the nut, then the shape is added to it, and therefore we can move up and down the fret board. Isn't it wonderful? Each time we do, a new Chord is formed. However, a price is paid for this convenience. As you know, Darlings, everything has its price. What we have here is a road that must be fully understood.

Not to go along with an empty mind, as a roadblock will occur if a pattern is not followed, and that is to know the notes along the way. That is our map to move along. This part is for the hardy, as it is not easy to forge ahead and absorb. However, on the other hand why the rush? The time will go by with or without us. That may sound cruel, but it is the fact of life. Time waits for no one. We could use it however we want, but please do not waste it.

The time really goes at a fast rate when the mind is serious, for as it moves along it is a onetime occurrence. Never to be repeated again. Once it is gone, that's it. Of course it seems too always be there, but this time around it is all new and fresh to use for whatever purpose we want. It also means we are a little bit older. If we concentrate, and intensify our efforts for short periods of time it will go a long way.

Now Dears, I am putting in a Guitar Chart on page 61 that happens to be present in the Vol. I. Page 30 of these Series. This will be a great help when you are memorizing. To play these Bar Chords it is best to know your way around the Fret Board. Otherwise it is like traveling in a foreign country. When we are in that period of time, it is just a fast look around. Not much is really absorbed, except a fragment here and there.

I'LL TAKE YOU HOME AGAIN, KATHLEEN

The A Chord is in its 2nd inversion that is where the C# comes from,
and the D Chord in its 1st inversion and the F# appears.

I'll TAKE YOU HOME AGAIN KATHLEEN

The Key of F with one flat is called Bb. When using a Chord as an Arpeggio for the introduction, more interest is added on if the Arpeggio, instead of playing the 5th degree of the scale, which C-E-G-, we are using C-E-G#. Then the piece starts as usual. The next Arpeggio is at the end of the piece. This time we use the one Chord, which is the F Chord, and that is F-A-C, without adding anything to it, as that is the final closing of the piece.

If you have a piece that you would like to try this introduction, please do, as it will give you some freedom of your talent. A good idea is to write it down on some music paper and then add the half step to the Chord. For instance, say you have a piece in the Key of G. This will be the Chord of G -B-D. We use the chord a 5th above which give D-F#-A. The last note of the chord is changed. The A is turned into an A#. It is then resolved at the end.

This is an enharmonic change. It is more relaxing as we go along to know what is happening. If a slight change takes place without the proper understanding, we could get agitated, and that can be upsetting.

I'll take you home again Kathleen 'Cross the ocean wild and wide, To where your heart has ever been Since first you were my bonny bride, The roses all have left your cheek. I've watched them fade away and die, Your voice is sad when e'er you speak, And tears bedim your loving eyes. Oh I will take you back Kathleen To

THE GUITAR VERSION

C | | | | F | | | |
where your heart will feel no | pain, And |

F | | | Bb | | |
when the fields are fresh and | green, I'll |

F | C | F | | |
take you to your home a- | gain. ‖

BAR CHORD

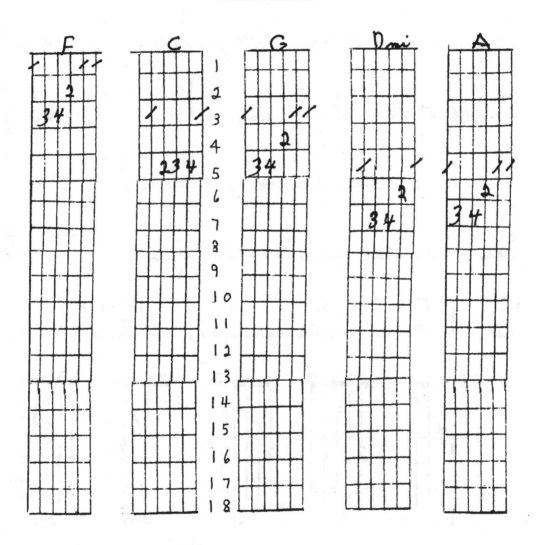

54

CHOPSTICKS

CHOPSTICKS SECONDO

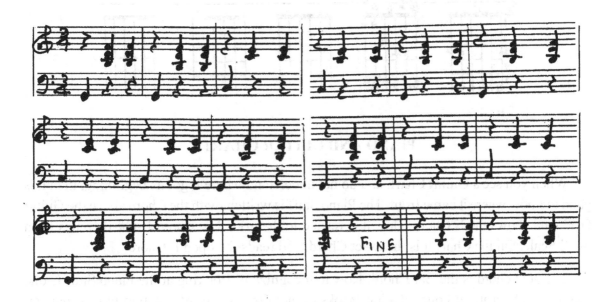

E BAR CHORD

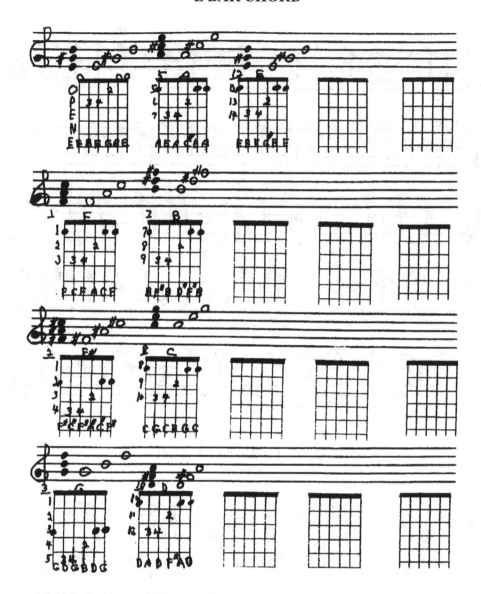

PIANO AND GUITAR CHART

When you see a Guitar Chart, and do not understand where it got its beginning, then it is good to know where it came from. The Piano Staff is written, with the Chord above the Guitar Grid, and shows the E Chord: How it is related to the grid. The Chord E-G#-B comes from the E Scale. On the Chart it is the exact Chord, and reads the open E Chord.

The next chord is the Bar Chord. How to recognize it! Looking at the Piano Staff is one way to go about it. Of course Guitar Books do not display the information in this manner. This is unusual to point out by going into it with more depth. Advanced players could easily transpose the piano chord into the proper grid, or have the option to play a plain E Chord, or play a Bar Chord.

ANALYZING BAR CHORDS

The first Chord above is E. This is called a Basic Chord. Notice that it has 3 open strings. A Bar Chord cannot have any open strings. In the next grid, place the 1st finger over the entire 1st fret, and then the Chord Shape, and a new chord is born. Believe it or not Darlings. But just to make sure let us prove it. The 1st finger is holding down all 6 strings. Starting from the 1st fret and 1st string it reads F. If it is an open string this would be E. Make it clear that this is how it is.

Continue to the 2nd string and still the 1st fret which reads C. Remember, when it was an open B. The 3rd string on the 2nd fret is A, and the 4th and 5th string on the 3rd fret reads: F and C, but we are not finished as the 1st finger is still holding down the 1st fret on the 6th string which reads F. So, Darlings this is now a Bar Chord, and is called by its proper name: An F Bar Chord.

Notice the Shape of the Chord that was used happened to be the original E Chord. What is amazing is that if we go up the Guitar in this manner we could derive a dozen or more chords like magic. By just going up the ladder, using this same E Chord and producing all of these Chords. Can you ask for anything more? Well, I guess so, but only if you are the inquisitive type. I believe which is the best way to be.

To play the next Chord-F#/Gb is a complex problem, but only if you let it be one. The usual way for most is just mindlessly climb the ladder. That is one way to reach the top, and the quick way, but leaving out all the juice. The other is by understanding what is going on. Everything has a pathway in life. Nothing is slapped together without a purpose.

Understanding this fine line makes learning a pleasure. Knowing the time is well spent in whatever is chosen to increase the process. Teaching the brain new information is hard work. It would be nice if it were easy, but because once the task is completed the proper way through exertion, and it helps if the interest is there. It will reward for a lifetime.

That is how great composers come into being. Their persistence is unique. Of course one could say talent has everything to do with it. But to go back in time one could say that is what gave them their talent. We just add onto it. Why would a person come into the world with a true plan? Where does it come from? Was it handed to us as a gift? Or, did we already do the work, and then continued on because it is part of us. That question will have to remain unanswered.

It is wonderful when we find our place, and are happy in it. It means we have arrived. There is much satisfaction in this thought. Now, Darlings let us get real. Back to the grind, and to further our knowledge, we must put the effort into it. A little bit each day goes a long way. Repeat what was done the day before, and you will see some of the work has really congealed. Then go a bit further and see if you can add to it.

MOVING THE E SHAPE BAR CHORD

Combining the Musical Staff of 5 lines and 4 spaces, with the Chord Diagrams on which Chords are written show that any instrument can be played from the same source. In other words looking at the staff can be applied to the interest of the instrument on hand. It is important to read music, as all of the information needed is there for use. Playing by ear (meaning, that a non-reading musician relies only on his ability to hear the right sound), is indeed very limited in that respect. It is best to expand the knowledge for further insight into a subject.

We will go over the aspect of what is going on. In looking at the complexity of the material, and to understand it more thoroughly is to step back and look at it with a clear mind. Can you blame some of the Rock Bands for grabbing a Guitar, and playing a few chords, and filling the rest with all kinds of antics added to it? That has to be added as the music is too sparse to hold any ones attention for long.

In going over the Chords, the open E Guitar Chord comes from the E Scale. To translate this into a Guitar Chord for the instrument, the grid is placed below, and then has the proper notes applied. The 6 strings of the Guitar are used and the E Chord is ready to play. The next grid on the 1st fret will be our Bar Chord. It has the same format, except a Bar Chord is placed in it. The piano staff above it has the F Chord, and is in the Key of F. We are still dealing with the Bar Chords, and the same E Shape will be used for the rest of the page to show how the process works.

The 2nd fret is an F# Bar Chord with the E shape. All of the notes are comprised from this Scale. If you do not know the Scale then how can you know the Chord? The Scales are all written out in Volume I. For now Bar the 1st finger over all the strings on this fret, and add the Shape of the E Chord. This is now called an F# Bar Chord. This is continued along these lines Darlings.

The 3rd fret on the 6th string is a G, and this gives the new Bar Chord. Use some of the time at the present moment to impress the mind of the changes that are taking place. What changes you might ask? You may not be aware of them, and if that is the case, not much has been recorded, so do make sure the awareness is alive and well.

Check the Guitar Chart only after you struggle for the right answer. For instance, if you are on a plane, or other means of transportation, and you select the 3rd fret to go over in your mind, and the right note doesn't show up, then open the Chart for a clue, then go back and push forward.

Feel free to tackle the 5th fret. This will be more difficult, as starting from this point, the first two strings will come easily, but then, here is where the going gets tough: the 3rd string will have the 2nd finger on the 6th fret, and it will be difficult to reach for the right answer. It means that the mind must go back to the fret above and remember what that was called. Is it any worse that a (Cross Word Puzzle). I think not.

Continuing onward, and to make clear the notes on the 5th fret. It is a good idea to move back a few frets for some balance. Looking at the Bar Chord Diagram, check out the 3rd fret and work up to the 5th. To know the notes on this fret, one way is to keep in mind the 3rd fret. If the 1st string reads G, then the 5th would be A. This is a whole note. In between G and A happens to be a # or a flat. If it is a whole note remember what is in between. If it is a half note, just move along. After the B, on the 7th fret is C, a half note which is on the 8th fret. These notes, B's and C's sail right through, and are a welcome sight to see.

It is more difficult when the notes move in whole steps. When the sharps and flats come into play it does require some deep thinking. If the musical alphabet is recited mentally what we get is a clear picture of where the whole and half steps occur. This is where the mental process comes into play: A-B-C-D-E-F-G. Clearly between B and C are the half notes. The next half note is E- F. That leaves 5 notes that are whole notes.

Let us start with the beginning of the 7 letters. This seems easy enough Darlings, but this is where the going gets tough. Starting with the 1st letter of A: could be A#, or A flat. The same with the 2nd letter of B, could be a B# or B flat. The 3rd is C. could be C# or C flat. The 4th could be D# or D flat. The 5th could be E# or E flat. The 6th could be F# or F flat. The 7th could be G# or G flat.

This is just the tip of the iceberg. Once you fall down the hill, there is no end in sight. It is endless. So, the moral of this story is not to get lost, but to stay on course. When the confusion sets in, so does the entanglement. It is best not to reach that stage. Understanding each bit of the endeavors is the way to go.

If looking at the Piano and the Guitar Chart (P. 56) causes a problem, this is the time to correct it. If the Guitar Chart is removed, and only the Piano one is left by itself, then any instrument can be played from this source. On the other hand if the reverse were to appear it would be very difficult to understand. Trying to get a clear picture of the situation is like doing double duty.

Having some knowledge of the Piano sets the groundwork for any other instrument, and that includes the Human Voice, and Percussion Instruments. Without this beginning it takes a much longer time to get to the juice of it all. But to be realistic, whatever stage we are in is what we have at the moment. Taking it from there, continue with the momentum on hand.

Try to keep a mental picture to impress upon the mind: The seat of it all. Learning the notes on the higher register of the Guitar is no easy task. One way is to introduce this to oneself by doing it in small bits. Go back to the frets that are familiar, as up to the 5th fret, and then move along to add a fret or two. Go slowly, and try to absorb the new knowledge on all of the 6 strings in the same fashion. By that I mean to learn the notes on the following 2 additional frets on these strings. They must become a part of your life, and to keep it that way is to do a little each day in the same time slot of your day.

CHAPTER EIGHT

*****

LESSON 8

CHORD CHART FOR GUITAR

Below is a Chord Chart of 15 frets on the Guitar. On the left side are the #'s. Starting with the first open string called E, then by pressing the fret down will cause the pitch to change to F. In memorizing this string if one has free mental time, do use it for this purpose. When one thinks of so many hours that a person falls into this abyss of time, it becomes appalling. Translation: a bottomless hole. It is hard to imagine such a place, but it does exist. It is also where one could hide from the world.

It is better to use such a situation to gain knowledge. Since it is available, why not use it. When this free time pops up, and it does quite frequently, as compared to the opposite such as in the movies, where things and people seem to always be running or cars exploding. It is strange that real life does not follow this plan. It is more static for most of the day, except when the mood forces the body to move for various reasons.

Like rushing for a train, and then finding a seat, and not move again maybe for hours. This seems to be the cycle of life. Only out of necessity does the body make a move. Most of the living is done with the brain. So, for this reason when finding yourself in this situation, do take your Chord Chart, and say the musical alphabet. Starting with the first string, skipping the #'s and flats for a moment. Relax and then say A-B-C-D and start the E string with F-G-A-B-C D-E-F. If stopped on the F, as with the starting point it comes to exactly 8 letters.

When that is set firmly in the mind go back and put in the #'s where they belong. If need be look at the chart, and then away from it, and see how right it was with the 5 #'s in their proper place. I feel it was found not to be as easy as thought at first. Notice that when reviewing, and this time looking at the chart, the letter names go in half steps except the B and C, and the E and F the starting point. For the B and C and the E and F are already half steps. All of the others were whole steps to begin with.

Now this turns out to be real detective work Darlings, as it should be. Once this is done a feeling of accomplishment takes place, and a feeling of well- being occurs, as of a job well done which deserves it to be.

CHORD CHART

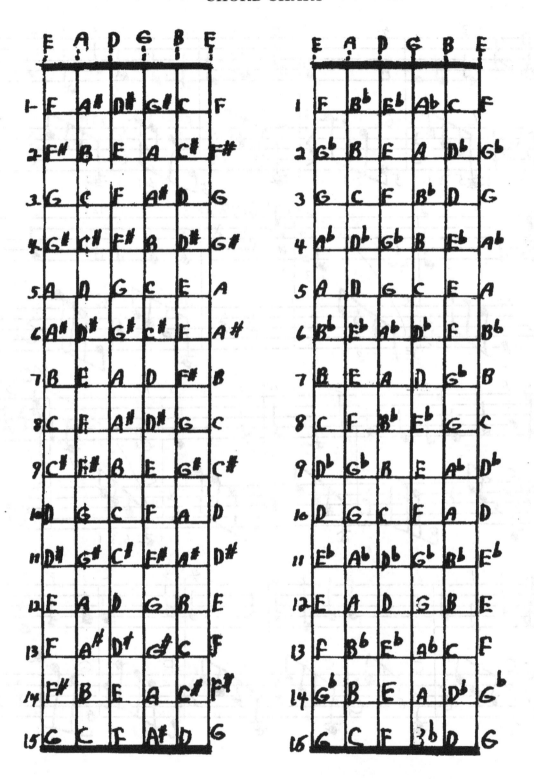

The Chord Chart shows 15 frets on the Guitar. A copy can be carried around at all times. It is like having an invisible instrument for your convenience. All of the frets are numbered to keep them in order.

DRINK TO ME ONLY WITH THINE EYES

DRINK TO ME ONLY WITH THINE EYES

This piece is in the Key of C. The left hand plays a broken C Chord. One way to practice with the left hand is to play a solid Chord, then play the note C one octave below: If in doubt look at the next C on the left side of the Piano. Once that is completed, then move the left hand without actually playing, but just move the hand from the low C to the Chord and do that a few times in silence. Here is where the mental aspect comes into play. Without the sound, the concentration is at its peak. Isn't that wonderful?

Adding the sound too soon, will take away the impression of playing with ease. Once the feeling of familiarity is accomplished, add the music. On the other hand if one plunges with false confidence expecting a brilliant performance, be prepared for a disappointment. It's not going to happen. Knowledge is the key to it all. I know some of the musicians reading this little bit of how to practice don't need any of this information, but Darlings we must not think everyone is so endowed.

Do notice that once this hurdle is out of the way, it is clear sailing. All of the 3 Chords, C-F-G have the same style. On the 7th and 8th measure, a change is definitely taking place, and that is the left hand crossing over the right to play part of the 2nd inversion of the C Chord. This occurs again on measures 15th and 16th, and again at the end of the piece. All of this mind work does make everything fall in place.

$\frac{3}{4}$

C / / | G / / | C / / | F / / |
Drink to me On - ly With Thine Eyes and

C / / | G / / | C / / | C / / |
I - will pledge with mine

C / / | G / / | C / / | F / / |
Or leave a kiss with in - the cup - and

C / / | G / / | C / / | C / / |
I'll - not ask for wine The

C / / | C / / | C / / | C / / |
thirst - that from the soul - doth rise doth

F / / | G / / | C / / | G / / | C / |
ask a drink di - vine but might I

G / / | C / / | F / / | C / / |
of Jove's nec - tar sup - I would - not

G / / | C / / | C / / |
change for thine

The C can be played with the open chord. You can change to the G as a Bar, and back to the C as open, and then the F as a Bar. As you feel more comfortable with Bar Chords, change the C at this point to the C on the 8th fret. Moving along in this fashion will help to memorize the Bar Chords.

Using them as often the opportunity occurs for best results. Keep in mind that the Bar Chords on the 6th string are all based on the open E major shape form, the same chord that is found on the Open E Chord. Using this system is certainly great to obtain at least 12 new chords. This depends on what type of Guitar one is playing.

A TIME TO PRACTICE

The serious musician must get seated at the instrument of choice. A determined and resolute person must set a time that is best suited to add to the list of what is expected when a new venture is introduced. If the days are so occupied that it is impossible to find an opening, then it is quite a problem. But everyone on this earth could find a space by doing some house cleaning.

In other words throw some things out that are unnecessary. Might be easier said than done is the first thought that comes to mind. There always is time for T.V. This is the worst offender. With so much waste of time just thinking about it, then take action and make the time by getting rid of at least one show.

Once this is done, then don't let go of this precious time, and use it because it is for a worthy cause. Isn't it wonderful to discover that this time existed? All we had to do was to take control of it. So, the time is there, now we have to make sure it doesn't disappear. Since time is not physical, it must be treated differently. Like for instance: with the utmost respect, almost unearthly, or shall we say with reverence.

If after a long day at work, and once in the easy chair, have the music right at hand, just reach over and spend a few minutes going over from the day before. It is important to keep this in order by adding, and connecting the whole unbroken series. More like reading a story; and it makes sense going forward from the day before, as the memory of what transpired, and then the continuation, and adding from that point does make it more interesting.

A Fiction Author for instance, must read all of the material that was typed in the day before. As making up a story, all of the threads of the plot must be firmly kept in mind. There is no way to continue with the intricate twists and turns of the plot without first reviewing what was put down yesterday. Can you imagine the chaos that would occur? I would venture to say enough to put one away in a sanitarium.

The question: is it any different with learning a new skill? Keeping this in mind, it is important to think in the same vein. The old fashion way of learning is to study a tit-bit of information, but having not much of a connection to the material that had existed the day before. Just jumping around without a continuation of attaching where one left off is very taxing on the brain. Doing this each day at study time makes it difficult to comprehend, and the interest is lost very quickly.

Not only that, but not much is gained, as each new bit of information seems to be foreign to what was seen yesterday. Knowing each day where one left off the day before is like seeing an old friend, and is welcomed as such. Otherwise, an unfriendly twist occurs when looking at this new page with all kinds of strange facts that doesn't seem to make any sense. This could also mean that the book we are looking at has flaws. It is best to have more than one book on hand, as the material may have skipped over some vital facts.

IN THE GLOAMING

The last measure on the previous does not have the Chords written in. This is a good time to try your skill in figuring out the B flat Chord on your own. Actually, I missed putting it in, but then thought I couldn't get away with it, because my musicians are too smart for a little bit of mishap. It just shows how one could untangle it, and use it in another manner.

The end of the piece has two endings. It shows how normally it would end with the double lines indicating the close of the music. However, in this case, on the bottom line we close with a flourish, using the same introduction that was used at the beginning. Do notice that even though they look alike, there is a difference. The closing must end in the Key it started with. In this case it is the Key of F. Of course, in ultramodern music a composer who throws everything in, could end it in any form he fancies, but would anyone listen to it? I doubt it would go very far.

GUITAR VERSION

At this point we will introduce another set of Bar Chords. This set is located on the 5th string, and will act in the same manner that was studied with the 6th string.

CHAPTER NINE

*****

LESSON 9

A SHAPE BAR CHORDS

The A Shape Bar Chord acquires its name from the 5th string. The process is the same, but, looking at the A Chord which consists of A-C# -E. has three different choices in picking the fingering. 3-2-1 is the normal fingering for the open A Chord. For the bar chord some use 3-3-3, however, the third choice is 4-3-2. I have all three written down.

The open A has the piano version above the Guitar Grid. This open chord is stationary. It stays put Darlings. Only the Bar Chords have the ability to travel around the Guitar. Isn't that wonderful! The great part of this is that like the E Bar Chord, the A Bar Chord could ring out 12 different Chords, just by using the A Shape of it. Isn't it better to know how all of this began, instead of just being in the dark?

Most Music Books when introducing some complicated material just happily skip over the whole thing, and say, "No need to go into how, or why this is, just keep moving along and continue as before. Well, with a whole chunk of missing information, how is that possible? It only makes it much worse by not knowing what it is all about. I know whenever I would see that phrase I would be very disappointed in being left out in the cold. I guess they were too lazy to explain it further, or if they could.

When we try to memorize, the most difficult part is in keeping it long enough to make an impression. If a problem occurs, and a passage is not understood, then don't even try to go forward. Have a clear picture of what you want before you place it in your mind. Of course repeating it a few times will help to seal it. Let's face it: a habit starts that way, going over a thought, especially if it is pleasant, like a thousand times for years and years it will become cemented in the mind, then you know thoughts are powerful, so let us use it in a positive way.

Life is not to be wasted. I could never understand when some people stand on corners for hours doing nothing, but passing time. It goes to show that even if nothing seems to be going on, in actuality it is alive and well. As long as we are breathing something is going on, but the real question is: What? It means that it is active and anxious to move along with the time. This may be enough for some, but for others it is not enough to be used in that manner.

PIANO AND GUITAR CHORDS

It is important to see how these two instruments relate to each other. As we look at the Piano Staff, and understanding its significance in how the Guitar Grids complement each other does indeed help our studies. Without going into the core of it all, how can we move along with peace of mind? So, Dears, take a little bit each day, and put the puzzle together. It is so perfect in how it all locks in, that it is a joy to behold.

Let us see the inner workings of it again. Go back to the beginning, of the 1ˢᵗ string, and start reviewing. We are going through the counting from the 1ˢᵗ string and the 1ˢᵗ fret, which is F, to the 5ᵗʰ fret that is A on this 1ˢᵗ string. This gives the F-F#-G-G#-A. This comes to Frets 1 to 5.

Do the 2ⁿᵈ string in the same manner. Remember, the open 2ⁿᵈ string is B. Now, by pressing down the 1ˢᵗ fret of this string becomes C Dears, don't lose me, we are still on the 2ⁿᵈ string for practice, then C#/Db-on the 2ⁿᵈ fret, next is D-on the 3ʳᵈ fret, and moving along D#/Eb-for the 4ᵗʰ fret, and then E. on the 5ᵗʰ fret. Memorize these new notes on the 2ⁿᵈ string all the way to the 5ᵗʰ fret.

Take notice it is safe to put into the mind. Focus on this. Plant in the mind these two new notes. Reinforce the new material, and if need be go back to the beginning of the 1ˢᵗ fret and go through all the stages of how the 1ˢᵗ fret moved to the 5ᵗʰ fret, and how it was named. Keeping those two strings in mind, move to the 8ᵗʰ fret. Instead of reviewing all the way from the 1ˢᵗ fret, start from the 5ᵗʰ fret since it has been introduced.

So, the 1ˢᵗ string on the 5ᵗʰ fret is A. That we know. All we have to do is find out what the name of the string on the 8ᵗʰ fret. How interesting! Keep in mind that each step on the Guitar Board is but a half step. This differs from the Piano, as the keys are intermingled with whole steps and half steps.

Count A on fret 5, of the 1ˢᵗ string, and move up a step and fret 6 turns into A#/Bb. This gives the brain a double dose of work to comprehend, and believe it or not it is difficult to hold onto. To have an extensive mental range is to be admired. This is where the intelligence is put into play. However, this must be exercised, just as physical exercise is to the body. The brain needs a special process to have a wide mental range to grasp ideas and hold them. But only by practice does this have a chance of coming about.

Moving along to the **7ᵗʰ fret on the 1ˢᵗ string is B**, and the **next is C.** Fix in the mind how we got to **the 8ᵗʰ fret, and is now called C.** By going over this very carefully, and not rushing through does save a lot of time. Having left off on the 5ᵗʰ fret of the 2ⁿᵈ string, and it being **E**, the same method is used to arrive on the **8ᵗʰ fret called G.** If you are on a bus or plane or other transportation, and want the time to whiz by, put your mind at work with something useful. It is best to take this in increments, and keep adding to it as we go along. If the new material is not understood, then the whole object goes out the window.

If you feel strong enough to continue in this fashion, please do Darlings. I however will keep moving along, as much more information needs to be attended to. When traveling, so much empty space is allotted as we sit and just gaze idly around. At this time, if nothing interesting pops up, and you are wide awake: What to do? The brain seems to feel as if it needs more attention, and will let you know by making you tense, this is when you strike back and give it what it needs. It most likely needs something tangible to munch.

THE STAR SPANGLED BANNER

THE STAR SPANGLED BANNER

THE STAR SPANGLED BANNER

The Star Spangled Banner is the National Anthem of the United States. It was written by Francis Scott Key and is sung to music composed by John Stafford Smith. In March, 1931, Congress officially approved the song as the national anthem. But the Army and the Navy had recognized "The Star Spangled Banner" as the national anthem long before Congress adopted it.

HOW THE SONG CAME TO BE WRITTEN

During the War of 1812, the British forces took prisoner William Beanes of Upper Marlborough, Md., and held him aboard a warship in Chesapeake Bay. Two Americas received permission from President James Madison to communicate with the British in an effort to have Beanes released. The men were Francis Scott Key, a lawyer, and John S. Skinner, both of Washington, D.C.

Key and Skinner boarded the warship just as the vessel was preparing to bombard Fort McHenry, which protected the city of Baltimore. The British agreed to release Beanes. But they held all three Americans on a U.S. prisoner-exchange boat at the rear of the British fleet until after the battle ended, so they could not reveal plans of the attack to patriots on shore.

The bombardment started on Tuesday, Sept. 13, 1814, and continued all that day and almost all night. Key and his friend knew that Fort McHenry had little defense. The prisoners paced the deck all night. Even when dawn came, they did not know who won the battle because the smoke and haze was so thick.

Suddenly, at 7 o'clock, a break in the mist cleared the view for a moment, and they saw the American flag still flying over the walls of the fort. Key was so excited that he wanted to express his feelings. He pulled an unfinished letter from his pocket and started writing verses. He wrote most of the words of the song in a few minutes. Later that day, the British released the Americans, and Key returned to Baltimore, where he finished the other stanzas. The poem was printed on handbills the next morning, and distributed in the city.

By government permission the United States flag flies continuously over Key's grave at Frederick, Md., and over Fort McHenry.

Playing the Piece

Most people are very unfamiliar with the anthem as far as the verses are concerned, even though the Public Schools drilled the anthem on a daily basis in the morning auditorium. I had often wished for an easy way to learn this wonderful piece of history. One thought comes to mind, and that is to frame the music, with the verses, and keep it on the wall in the home or office.

Having the piece in the Key of C makes it easier to play and also to feel at ease when learning the verses. There are 4 changes of Chords: C-F-G-and D minor. Just looking at it and singing the melody inwardly is rather relaxing to do. I'm sure the words would have to be refreshed as we go along. But at this time just sing the melody and it becomes rather a pleasant experience.

Because this music has become part of every person in America, and is known and very familiar around the world, but not complete in its entirety as far as the words are concerned. For now, complete the music, and then in a second go around add the words as best as can be remembered. I doubt all of the verse will be in tip-top shape. It should be interesting to note where the memory faltered. So, just as a reminder the verse is here to solve the problem.

On the next page is the Guitar Version, with the words written out. When you are traveling, or resting in a recliner, and having the music books close on hand, add this most important music to be part of the whole process. Since it is a verse, it would be best to learn it without the music. Going at it with the completed version certainly makes it much more difficult to impress on the mind. Taking it apart does help to retain it.

By adding the music too soon makes it a hardship to continue. Once the verse is intact then blend the whole process together and just sail along. It is quite an accomplishment once this is achieved and one feels proud to be an American.

THE STAR SPANGLED BANNER

GUITAR VERSION

The chords can be played using the open version, or combining them with the Bar Chords. Since we are in the Key of C, and the C Bar Chord is on the 8th fret of the 6th string, and the G Bar chord is on the 3rd fret of the same string, an open chord could be played using the C. But, Darlings we could learn more Bar Chords at this time, and combine them for easier playing.

CHAPTER TEN

*****

LESSON 10

CIRCLE OF FIFTHS

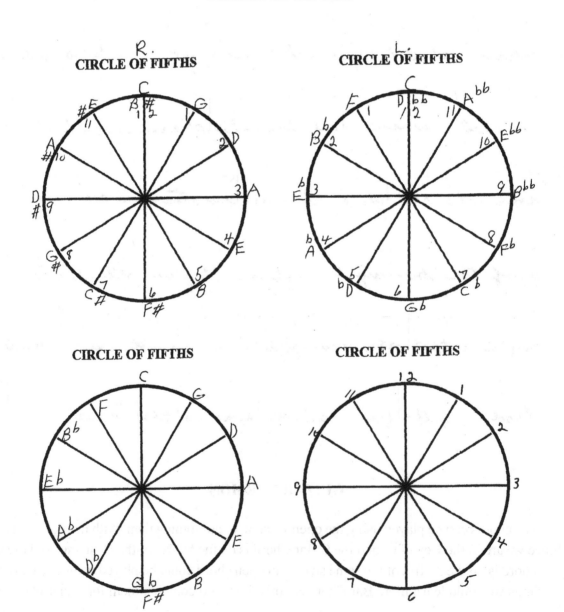

The Circle of Fifths works like a Clock. Taking the C Scale, starting at the top of the Clock at 12, and working from the right side around the Clock it will come back to the starting point of 12. It seems amazing, but it is a perfect arrangement. Try it with another key. Make a circle of a clock and number the top 12 and the other numbers. Then start with another key and see how it works. I will do another so as not to forsake you.

In continuing with the scales, and turning them into the Circle of Fifths write down the scale first, or it you feel it could done mentally, more power to you. Using the empty circles start with the scale of C then count up 5 from the C for the G scale. I decided to do a few of them, and put the answers on another page to make sure they are correct, and leave no doubt in the mind in that respect, Darlings.

In forging ahead in order of the scales, the next is D-A-E-B-F#-C#. What is so great with the circle is that it revolves like the wheel that it is. Like the moon revolves around the earth. It seems everything on the Earth is well planned. Nothing is by chance Dears. It is what it is. An author said: "OH EARTH DO YOU KNOW HOW WONDERFUL YOU ARE? DO PEOPLE REALLY APPRECIATE YOU?"

In looking at the scales do notice that as each new scale appears it has one more sharp added on than the one before it. Look carefully as you will also notice that the last half of each scale becomes the first half of the next scale. This happens with the sharps keys.

C-D-E-F	G-A-B-C	C D E F G A B C	1 2 3 1 2 3 4 5
G-A-B-C	D-E-F#-G	G A B C D E F# G	1 2 3 1 2 3 4 5
D-E-F#-G	A-B-C#-D	D E F#G A B C# D	1 2 3 1 2 3 4 5
A-B-C#-D	E-F#-G#-A	A B C#DE F# G# A	1 2 3 1 2 3 4 5
E-F#-G#-A	B-C#-D#-E	E F# G# A B C# D#E	1 2 3 1 2 3 4 5
B-C#-D#-E	F#-G#-A#-B	B C# D# E F# G# A# B	1 2 3 1 2 3 4 5
F#-G#-A#-B	C#-D#-E#-F#	F# G# A# B C# D# E# F#	2 3 4 1 2 3 1 2
C#-D#-E#-F#	G#-A# B#-C#	C#-D#-E#-F#-G#-A#-B#-C#	2 3 1 2 3 4 1 2
G#-A#-B#-C#	D#-E#-F+-G#	Ab-Bb-C-Db-Eb-F-G-Ab	2 3 1 2 3 1 2 3
D#-E#-F+G#	A#-B#-C+-D#	Eb-F-G-Ab-Bb-C-D-Eb	3 1 2 3 4 1 2 3
A#-B#-C+-D#	E#-F+-G+-A#	Bb-C-D-Eb-F-G-A-Bb	4 1 2 3 1 2 3 4
E#-F+-G+-A#	B#-C+-D+-E#	F-G-A-Bb-C-D-E-F	1 2 3 4 1 2 3 4
B#- C+- D+-E#	F+-G+-A+-B#	C-D-E-F-G-A-B-C	1 2 3 1 2 3 4 5
F+- G+- A+-B#	C+-D+-E+-F+	G-A-B-C-D-E-F#-G	1 2 3 1 2 3 4 5
C+- D+- E+-F+	G+-A+-B+C+	D- E- F#- G-A-B-C#-D	1 2 3 1 2 3 4 5

Notice that after the C# with the 7sharps. It seems to look like the end of the story. No such luck Dears. There is no end, the Universe doesn't work that way; it goes on forever. After the C#, the journey continues. It is rather refreshing to realize this. Who wants an ending? Life also works in that fashion. It goes on in a never-ending circle. The circle seems to be the Key to it all.

Music is part of every aspect of life. It cannot be separated. It doesn't matter what type of music is played. Music is a basic social and cultural activity of mankind. It has probably existed in some form from the earliest days of man. Man was born with a great musical instrument, his voice. He used this great gift to express himself, long before he thought of making music with instruments.

HE'S GOT THE WHOLE WORLD IN HIS HANDS

The bass is left empty so as to fill in with either the Guitar or Piano. If using the Guitar the Bar Chords would come in handy, as with only two chords the D, on the 5th string and the A7 on the 6th both land on the 5th fret.

INTRODUCTORY RUNS (ARPEGGIOS)

These are broken chords, and can be used on any chord, and played at the beginning of a song, or at the end. In this instance, as an example, in looking at the piece, we find that it is in the Key of G. Also it is in 2 quarter time, having 2 beats per measure. The chords are as follows: G-D7-C-A7.

In the last measure is a half circle with a dot in the middle called Fermata (far mah tah). It means to hold or pause, to hold longer than the normal duration. Next to it is D.C. Da capo (dah kah poh) means go back to the beginning of the piece and play a second time.

As far as chords are concerned: The Elementary Chords consist of 5 types. The chords are as follows: Major-Minor-Augmented-Seventh-and-Diminished. Of course, Darlings, we won't go into the ocean of Chords that run into the thousands like some Guitars Books have over 20,000. Perish the thought!!! That is enough to end this section for now. Sorry.

Speaking of this massive amount of chords reminds me of some Musicians that maybe have about as many as can be counted on the fingers. As far as their repertoire is concerned it is quite limited. Many make a living with just enough to get by. Of course other Musicians wouldn't think of having such a meager amount.

On the other hand, if it is overdone to subject a student to excessive amounts of chords to give the impression that this is necessary to be a Guitarist is not natural. It also borders on fraud. Many of the chords are just repeats, used over and over again. It looks good, but it is also frightening to phantom.

A Major Chord consists of a Major 3rd, and a Minor 3rd.
A Minor Chord consists of a Minor 3rd, and a Major 3rd.
A Dominant Seventh Chord consists of a Major 3rd plus two Minor thirds.
Augmented Chord: to change a Major Chord into an augmented raise the 5th a half step.
A Diminished Seventh Chord consists of 3 minor thirds.

If these Chords are not firmly set in the mind, the question is: how can one learn 22,000 chords for the Guitar? The answer is self-explanatory. It can't be done without great confusion. Once that happens the mind is all boggled up with misunderstanding: Enough to forget about going any further with the studies.

Knowing where the chords come from is quite enlightening, as it should be. Having them printed without giving the vital information is the name of the game to keep the confusion alive. Buy more books!

ANALYZING THE A SHAPE BAR CHORD

On page 70 is a Chart of the A Shape Bar Chords. Above the Guitar Grids is the Piano Version. This is where it pays off to know how to play the piano. If a Student starts guitar lessons as a first instrument, and never had piano lessons, it makes it very difficult to understand what is going on. No kidding! It is sad, but true. Once the mystery of music is revealed, then all that one does is apply it to any other instrument of interest.

Of course, this opens up a whole new field. The instrument in question must have the musical knowledge transferred to it. But can you imagine how this comes about? I would say by leaps and bounds. What a wonderful way to start learning something new that starts out as a blank A piano represents the most highly developed means of satisfying musical needs within a single instrument.

It can produce both melody and harmony at the same time. Its range covers almost all the sounds used in music. Pianists can play as soloists with an orchestra, as part of an orchestra, as part of smaller chamber-music groups, or as soloists. Of course some musical person may not agree with me, as a person likes and dislikes come into play.

I had studied classical guitar in New York, and my instructor told me when he found out that I played the piano he said, "I can't stand the piano, I don't like the sound of it, the guitar is an instrument with a sound that is just right." I guess after playing the classical guitar for most of his life one can come to that conclusion. It is true that the guitar is a beautiful instrument, and just about every 2nd person plays a guitar, easy to carry around. One could play it anywhere, and make music with very little knowledge. A lot of determination, and push, has made (for some) millions in the process.

Now, to the A Shape Bar Chords. It works the same way as the E Shape Bar Chords. The E shape had its root on the 6th string. The A shape will have its root on the 5th string. Follow the same pattern: play the open A string which is written below the Piano Chart The next chord will be the A#/Bb. Check out both instruments, as this chord will be the same with the exception by pressing all 5 string on the 1st fret will now appear as the A#/Bb chord.

On the Guitar Bar Chord Chart, it shows where to put the fingers to produce this new chord. By following this procedure will be the correct way to continue, if some confusion occurs go to page 61 for the Chord Chart, and this should clear things up for clarification. It is important to know these two Bar Chord Roots for they can produce what is needed to continue forward.

The open chords and the Bar Chords can be intermingled at the discretion of the performer. This does indeed give freedom to break out of the mold. Practice both ways, and see if this does enhance the beauty of the piece.

CIRCLE OF FIFTHS

CIRCLE OF FIFTHS

R.

CIRCLE OF FIFTHS

L.

CIRCLE OF FIFTHS

CIRCLE OF FIFTHS

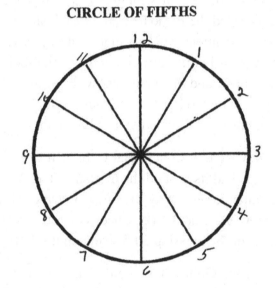

B-C#-D#-E	F#-G#-A#-B	Cb-Db-Eb-Fb-Gb-Ab-Bb-Cb	1 2 3 1 2 3 4 5
F#-G#-A#-B	C#-D#-E#-F#	Gb-Ab-Bb-Cb-Db-Eb-F-Gb	2 3 4 1 2 3 1 2
C#-D#-E#-F#	G#-A#-B#-C#	Db-Eb-F-Gb-Ab-Bb-C-Db	2 3 1 2 3 4 1 2

The B scale and the Cb scale show the Enharmonic Change- Ditto- for the F#, and C#.

In reviewing P.76 is to look at the scales in a new light. Many musicians have a very narrow view of scales and chords. Many Guitars players are satisfied with the knowledge of strumming a few chords, and live in the mystery of where they came from, and really don't care where they originated. It is interesting as one gets deeper into the field of music as knowing there must be an answer to how it moves along.

Enharmonic Scales are written differently, but they sound the same, and indicate the same Keys. It is a good idea to do this mentally to impress the mind to absorb this information, and store it where it is best held. When need be, it will always be available. As stated in the Circle of Fifths with the sharps, it will be noticed, the last half of the scale forms the first half of the following scale.

In reviewing this information, have the printed form to check as we go along. Start with the C Scale on top of the circle with the number 12. The next scale in order is G. This is where the first sharp appears. The scale of G has one #, which is called F#. This Circle of Fifths is moving in Fifths, as it moves to the Right of the Circle. Next to the G is the number 1 meaning the first # appears in the Key of G.

Next is D with the number 2, showing that there are two #'s. At the 3' O'CLOCK of the real time machine, in our clock it reads A with the number 3 showing the number of #'s. So, the Key of A has 3 #'s, also, notice this time machine is moving in Fifths. Next, is E with the number 4, which has 4 #'s. Keep going in this direction. 5'O'CLOCK has 5 #'s. being in the Key of B. On the half hour of the real time it is 6, on our time it is F# with 6 #'s. Moving along on the 7 O' CLOCK is indeed the 7 #'s in the Key of C #.

Now we have at the hour of 8, the Key of G # with 8 #'s. Following that comes the 9#'s of the Key of D# on the hour of 9 O'CLOCK, 10 O'CLOCK with 10 #'s from A#. 11 O'CLOCK the E# Scale with 11 #'s and finally at 12 O' CLOCK with the B# (enharmonic change). We started with the C and ended with the C. Isn't it wonderful Darlings?

In the Key of C, it works so perfectly, but it also does in the other keys. Since the pattern does not change. This only goes to show that the Universe is certainly in line of all things, yet our world is but a small part of the vastness that is hard to comprehend. The wonder is that knowledge is priceless. This gift is for all to tune in free of charge.

Alas, most people do not take advantage of all that is offered to us. Probably, because, our job is to realize we must take only what is needed, and not drown in the sea of boundless space. Go in on what is important, and add to our betterment. Of course this is easier said than done, but to be aware as we journey through life, and help the path that has been chosen for us.

FURTHER NOTES ON THE CIRCLE

The Sharps go around the Circle like a normal Clock, however, with the flats it goes around on the Left side. Starting on the top at 12 with the same C, but now we will go the opposite way (counter clockwise). Counting 5 from C, going left will give us the Key of F, which has one flat, and that is Bb. From the Key of F, counting 5 down to the Left gives the Scale of Bb, which has 2 flats. The third one is Eb with 3 flats. The fourth is Ab with 4 flats. Continuing in this fashion, count 5 to the left of the clock, will give the Db with 5 flats, and then Gb with 6 flats.

This brings us to the half hour of our clock. After the Gb, comes Cb with the 7b's, this time moving upwards to the right, to the Fb with 8b's. The next one is Bbb with 9b's. Remember that a Double sharp counts the same as two single sharps, and also a double flat counts the same as two single flats. No.10 is Ebb, followed by 11 with Abb, and 12 is Dbb, also called C (Enharmonic Change). We have reached full circle.

The third circle is the one that is in use at the present time, because it has been determined that the keys having more than six sharps, or six flats are too complicated in notation. Instead, the sharps keys are used for the first half of the circle from C to F#, and the flat keys are used for the second half to complete the round. The change is made at the F# to Gb (Enharmonic Change) on the half hour of the clock.

We start fresh with the clock. The first half starts with the C-G-D-A-E-B-F#. Once the F# is reached it becomes also Gb. From this point it turns into the flat keys. Let us begin with the top C. going down on the left side. This is the same as the second circle on p.76. After the C is F-Bb- Eb- Ab- Db- and the Gb. Knowing this information, does help in understanding the Scales, and that is knowledge that is indispensable to our studies in the music field.

RELATED KEYS

In the Circle of fifths each key is related to the one before it, because one half is found in that scale. It is also related to the one following it. Since the other half will be found in that one. The key of C is related to not only to the key of G, but also to the key of F. Let us see how that comes about.

C-D-E-F   G-A-B-C   We will go into the Flats Keys now.
G-A-B-C   D-E-F#-G

The last half of the sharps keys, as you recall, Dears, becomes the first half of the next key. In the case of the flats, it is reversed. So, Darlings, keep this in mind. **THE FIRST HALF OF THE FLAT KEYS, becomes THE LAST HALF OF THE NEXT KEY.** I hope this news does not upset you too much, as we can overcome it.

F-G-A-Bb	C-D-E-F	Key of F	F-G-A-Bb 1 2 3 4	C-D-E-F 1 2 3 4
Bb-C-D-Eb	F-G-A-Bb	Key of Bb	Bb-C-D-Eb 2 1 2 3	F-G-A-Bb 1 2 3 4
Eb-F-G-Ab	Bb-C-D-Eb	Key of Eb	Eb-F-G-Ab 3 1 2 3	Bb-C-D-Eb 4 1 2 3
Ab-Bb-C-Db	Eb-F-G-Ab	Key of Ab	Ab-Bb-C-Db 2 3 1 2	Eb-F-G-Ab 3 1 2 3
Db-Eb-F-Gb	Ab-Bb-C-Db	Key of Db	Db-Eb-F-Gb 2 3 1 2	Ab-Bb-C-Db 3 4 1 2
Gb-Ab-Bb-Cb	Db- Eb-F-Gb	Key of Gb	Gb-Ab-Bb-Cb 2 3 4 1	Db-Eb-F-Gb 2 3 1 2
Cb-Db-Eb-Fb	Gb-Ab-Bb-Cb	Key of Cb	Cb-Db-Eb-Fb 1 2 3 1	Gb-Ab-Bb-Cb 2 3 4 5

Fb-Gb-Ab-Bbb	Cb-Db-Eb-Fb	Key of Fb	Fb-Gb-Ab-Bbb 1 2 3 1	Cb-Db-Eb-Fb 2 3 4 5
E-F#-G#-A-E	B-C#-D#-E	Key of E	Enharmonic Change	

Give attention to the fact that the 4th note of the flats, is also the beginning of the next scale. Keep in mind, in addition, that we are working with only 7 different letters. A, B, C, D, E, F, G, so of course they are bound to come up with a never ending occurrence. This may be why it is so difficult for some to sort it out, whereas for others they may not be so aware of it which might be for the best.

It is amazing how much knowledge the human brain can obtain. It is the "Master Organ of the Body." The brain stores information from past experiences. If scientists could design an Electronic Computer to do the work of one human brain, the computer would be the size of the Empire State Building.

So, Darlings, be proud in knowing that the time is not wasted in learning new endeavors. This is something that also must be kept in mind, and that is to put only good knowledge in for its permanence. Since time is limited on this Earth, it is best to use it wisely. Some people are born knowing exactly why they were put on this Planet. Others are not quite sure, but perhaps have an inkling, and some don't have a clue. Our job is to find our true place, and forge ahead.

It seems the reason music is so wide spread in this Universe, is because we are all born with it. Each in varying degrees and depending on how high the interest happens to be then that will be our guiding light. From that point on it will take care of itself, and lead us onward. All that is left for us to do is follow our dreams. If the interest is not full blown to that extent, then it could be a secondary career, which is still awesome.

Not to be a jack-of-all-trades, one must avoid at all costs. It is OK to have hobbies, but one must distinguish between the two. One is something that comes and goes. To relinquish when other interests appear, that is what makes things interesting, trying different aspects. It is fun to get a taste of this and that. That is how we learn to improve ourselves, but a Life Career, brings a course of action for life, is something that does stay for life.

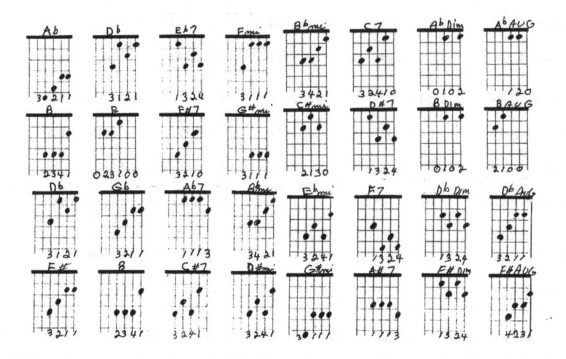

I decided to make the Chords more complete, and give a chance for the ones beginning on P.20, to digest it more completely. This way it will not overwhelm, but even welcome it for the additional information. We started with the C Chord, which comes from the C Scale. When an interval of a Third and a Fifth are formed, it is called a Triad. This Triad is now called a Chord, containing 3 notes. Triads are divided into four kinds: Major, Minor, Diminished, and Augmented.

Major Chord:	C-E-G	1 3 5	Using the Key of C as an example.
Minor Chord:	C-Eb-G	1-b3-5	
Diminished Chord:	C-Eb-Gb	1-b3-b5	
Augmented Chord:	C-E-G#	1-3-#5	

Starting with the C Chord, and then the F Chord, and a G7th, and again the C is the usual order for an ending of a piece of music. This is called the 1-1V-V7-1 or Resolution-meaning that, "The harmony of a whole from a dissonance to a consonance is resolved." When a piece of music comes to an end, it can't be left up in the air; it yearns for an ending of the piece. This is where the 1-1V-V-or V7-1 comes into play. A sample using the C Chord has been used.

These three chords: Tonic, Dominant, and Sub-dominant are called the Principal or the Primary Triads. **They contain every note of the scale.** The Triads on the remaining degrees are called Secondary Triads.

We have the Circle of Fifths Dears, so as to start trying to fill them up. With all the different Scales that are at our choosing, we will need more of them, so feel free to add as you move along. It is a great way to use the scales in this manner, and quite interesting to see the inner working of how they are constructed.

COME, THOU ALMIGHTY KING

Until we meet again I will leave you with the best that Life has to bless upon you. Continue with your music, and add your own personality, whichever way you feel will enhance it. It has been a joy to be part of this wonderful experience. Add new pieces, and try your new skills, which I'm sure has climbed ahead to give you a great push to further a feeling of accomplishment.

Mary Sewall

About the Author

MARY SEWALL is a member of the "New York State Music Teachers Association".

Brooklyn Conservatory of Music—"Diploma Graduate"

Chartered by the Regents of the University of the State of New York.

The Music School of the "Henry Street Settlement"—Award for Excellence.